D1580330

Created by WavemStudios

Book design by Michael Fletcher

Printed and bound in Spain

ISBN 978-1-5272-2124-6

"Business is War"

Jack Tramiel

STEVEN FLETCHER
FILMMAKER & PROGRAMMER

My name is Steven Fletcher and I'm a documentary filmmaker but most of my working life I've been a computer programmer.

For me the love affair of the computer started at the age of 14 when I got my first computer the VIC-20, closely followed by the Commodore 64 and then of course the Amiga.
Now 35 years later I want to take you on a journey back to the birth of the home computer by following the Commodore story; discovering the origins and what lead up to the Commodore 64 being the best ever selling computer in history.

It's remarkable that in my lifetime technology has advanced so much from computers once the size of a room to mobile phones that fit in your pocket.

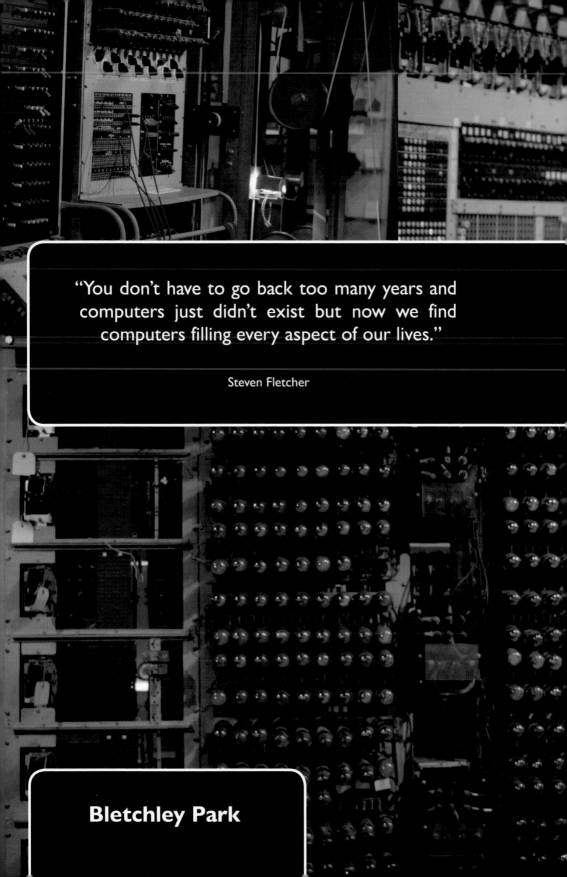

"You don't have to go back too many years and computers just didn't exist but now we find computers filling every aspect of our lives."

Steven Fletcher

Bletchley Park

Just arriving in San Francisco.
We're going to be doing the Commodore Story documentary
and the first thing we see is from a museum and it's all about
the typewriter. Potentially the first chapter, the first part of
the documentary we are going to call 'The Typewriter Man'
because it's all about Jack Tramiel and
where he came from.

Steven Fletcher

UNITED STATES OF AMERICA

MEXICO

THE BAHAMAS

CUBA

HAITI DOMINICAN
REPUBLIC

JAMAICA PUERTO
RICO

SAINT KITTS AND NEVIS

MONTSERRAT
GUADELOUPE

DOMINICA

BELIZE

MARTINIQUE

GUATEMALA

HONDURAS

EL SALVADOR

SAINT VINCENT BARBADOS

NICARAGUA

TRINIDAD AND TOBAGO

SAN JOSE

PANAMA

VENEZUELA

GUYANA

SURINAME

COLOMBIA

FRENCH

GALAPAGOS

ECUADOR

ICELAND

FAROE ISLANDS

SWEDEN

FINLAND

NORWAY

ESTONIA

LATVIA

LITHUANIA

IRELAND

UNITED
KINGDOM

DENMARK

NETHERLANDS

BELGIUM

LUXEMBOURG

GERMANY

POLAND

BELARUS

CZECH REP.

SLOVAKIA

UKRAINE

LIECHTENSTEIN

SWITZERLAND

AUSTRIA

HUNGARY

MOLDOVA

FRANCE

SLOVENIA

CROATIA

ROMANIA

BOSNIA
AND

PORTUGAL

SPAIN

ITA

URK

ZORES (PORTUGAL)

CYPRUS

LEB

MADEIRA ISLAND (PORTUGAL)

TUNISIA

CANARY ISLANDS (SPAIN)

WESTERN
SHARAH

MAURITAI

"We will also be attending Commodore and
Amiga events plus retro shows to see how
alive the Commodore and Amiga scene is in
today's modern world.
We will be travelling around Europe and
across America interviewing many legends
from Commodore and Amiga."

CAPE VERDE

SENEGAL

THE GAMBIA

GUINEA-BISSAU

GUINE

SIERRA LEONE

LIBERIA

COTE
D'IVOIRE

GHANA

CENTRAL
AFRICAN
REPUBLIC

CAMEROON

BIOKO (EQUATORIAL GUINEA)

EQUATORIAL GUINEA

SAO TOME

GABON

DEMOCRATIC
REPUBLIC

RWANDA

UGAN

"A half a million dollars, March 7th 1984."

Leonard Tramiel

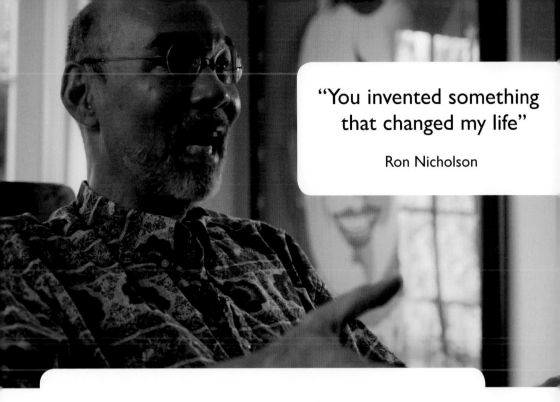

"You invented something that changed my life"

Ron Nicholson

"And there's a bunch of Z8000 programmers looking like I just shot a sheep or something."

Bil Herd

"On the other side rather than panicking because your ball grid array or something was inverted and there's nothing you can do about it."

Dave Haynie

Michael Tomczyk

A meeting with Jack Tramiel was often called a 'Jack attack'

"Do you ever get a jump where it's ten times better these days? – no"

Jeff Porter

"Welcome to RJ Mical's house of construction."

R J Mical

ACT 1
THE TYPEWRITER MAN

LEONARD TRAMIEL
COMMODORE (SON OF BOSS)

My name's Leonard Tramiel and I was involved in the personal computer industry for quite some time.

I was on the team that developed the Commodore PET and then actually went off to graduate school and didn't have any direct involvement in the VIC-20 or Commodore 64.

I had some indirect work with some of the engineers and marketing folk and of course with my dad.

The way Commodore got into the computer business was completely by accident.

So let's take a couple of historical steps back.

My father when he left the US army had some experience repairing typewriters; he was trained to do that in the army. One of his first jobs after leaving was he got the contract to continue doing the typewriter repair for the army base. His business went from repairing typewriters to importing and selling typewriters. Then from typewriters into other office equipment like adding machines and then from adding machines to electronic calculators.

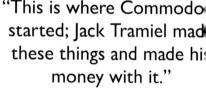

Ate van der Meer

I have an interesting story about this piece of equipment. Everybody knows that Jack Tramiel didn't really have a lot of interest in the computer business; he wanted to sell calculators like this one.
And a lot of people will recognise this specific chiclet keyboard.
It was Chuck Peddle who engineered the first computer for Commodore but because real keyboards were really expensive at the time Jack Tramiel designed it as this keyboard.

"This is where Commodo[re] started; Jack Tramiel mad[e] these things and made hi[s] money with it."

Marvin Droogsma

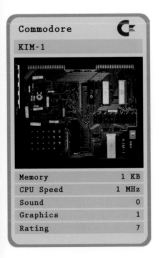

Commodore	
KIM-1	

Memory	1 KB
CPU Speed	1 MHz
Sound	0
Graphics	1
Rating	7

Virtually every calculator was designed around a calculator chip produced by Texas Instruments and our friends at TI decided that they wanted to get into the calculator business. So they produced calculators and sold them for roughly the cost that they were selling the calculator chip for, which drove everybody out of business.

My father said; so he told this story a couple of times; he said that in his mind his reaction was 'well they can die but I'm not going to die that easily'. Being a holocaust survivor survival was an important thing for him.

He found a calculator chip company or a company that made calculator chips and it turned out they were not doing all that well financially and so he bought them. One of the projects that this company was involved in was a little thing that he knew nothing about called the microprocessor. The MOS technology 6502, which was probably the most used microprocessor of all time.

All the Commodore machines in that series, the PET, the VIC-20 and Commodore 64, all of those. All of the Apple 8-bit machines, all of the Atari 8-bit machines, including the Atari video entertainment system and the Nintendo machine all used that same chip, which is really quite amazing.

How do you make it work?

You've got to have some programming going along with it. It needs to have some memory; needs to have some I/O. So Chuck designed the KIM, which is Keyboard Interface Module if I remember correctly.

It had a 16-button keyboard that allowed you to enter commands, to program the thing in Assembly language or actually in binary in hexadecimal code.

It was lots of fun because that's the way all programming should be done. That was the first personal computer I ever used, I had a KIM in my bedroom.

Andy Finkel was the Software Manager from the early 80's to 1994

Andy Finkel

MOS Technology was in Norristown and I'd actually visited MOS Technology when I was in high school. I met Chuck Peddle and bought a KIM 1 directly from the factory. So Commodore, since they owned MOS technology, I figured would be a perfect fit for me. So when Neil gave me a call I applied and got a job with the VIC-20 team, headed by Michael Tomczyk.

Leonard Tramiel

Chuck had designed the chip as a first step in a process where he wanted to make; and this is going to sound pretty funny; he wanted to make household robots a thing. The first thing he needed was a really inexpensive microprocessor and so he met with my dad. He said "I'm going to make this computer, if you want Commodore to make this computer I'll work for you and Commodore will make this computer". Dad said, "Ok, let me think about it" and he came home and spoke to me and said, "I have no idea what he's talking about. Come meet this guy, talk to him about it and tell me what you think".

So this punk kid at twenty goes to meet the designer of what is probably one of most influential pieces of technology ever; Chuck Peddle, the designer of the 6502. Chuck and I sit down in a booth at an embedded computer system fair. They had as an example of a marvellous thing that you can build with this; a pinball machine. Chuck and I sit down to talk about computers and we spent most of the time talking about science fiction.

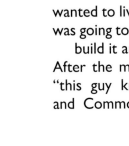

It was a science fiction story by Robert Heinlein called 'The Door Into Summer'; which is all about a world full of personal computers and Chuck wanted to live in that world. So if no one else was going to make that world he was going to build it and the first step was the PET.

After the meeting I talked to dad and said, "this guy knows what he's talking about" and Commodore went into the computer business.

Commodore	C=
PET	
Memory	4-96 KB
CPU Speed	1 MHz
Sound	0
Graphics	2
Rating	9

"I joined Commodore in 1981 in the United Kingdom despite this American accent."

GAIL WELLINGTON
COMMODORE & AMIGA

Commodore/Amiga 1 to 1994. Head of Spe Projects, Manage CATS (Commodore Ar Technical Sup

"My first computer was the Commodore VIC-20. I was six years old when I got that."

DAVID MURRAY
THE 8 BIT GUY

"I managed to augment my meagre savings and we went out and bought a second hand Commodore 64 for my birthday."

Kenny is the Academi Curriculum Manager for th School of Arts, Media an Computer Games at th University of Aberta

KENNY MCALPINE
8 BIT MUSIC EXPERT

"My first computer started with the Commodore 64."

Mark Barrett

"I got my first computer, home computer, which was the Commodore 64."

Robert Bernardo

Dan Wood

"I remember Christmas morning 1988, I think it was, I unwrapped a Commodore Plus/4."

Commodore

Plus/4

Com

Plus

Com

Plus

Co

P

64 KB

Memory   1.76 Mhz

CPU Speed   5

Sound

Graphics

Rating

Sound

ics

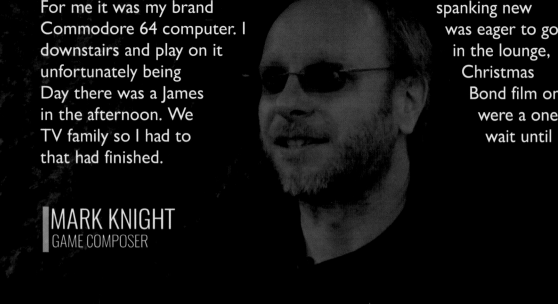

For me it was my brand [...] spanking new
Commodore 64 computer. I [...] was eager to go
downstairs and play on it [...] in the lounge,
unfortunately being [...] Christmas
Day there was a James [...] Bond film or
in the afternoon. We [...] were a one
TV family so I had to [...] wait until
that had finished.

MARK KNIGHT
GAME COMPOSER

Also known as TDK and Madfiddler, Mark is a British video game music composer,
sound designer, chiptine composer, and electric violinist.

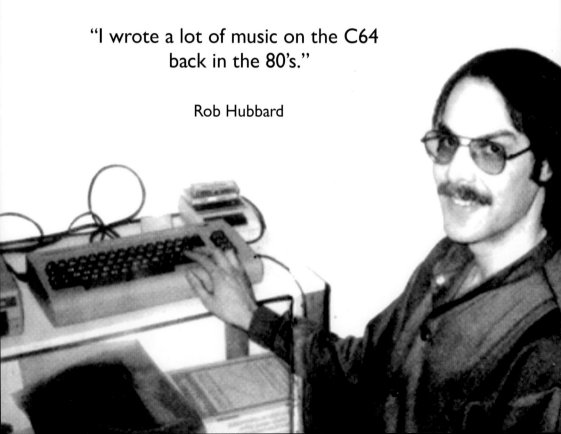

"I wrote a lot of music on the C64
back in the 80's."

Rob Hubbard

SERAFIN FUENTE
C64 USER

Serafin Fuente

"We are here in Atlanta, Georgia and my first computer was the Commodore 64."

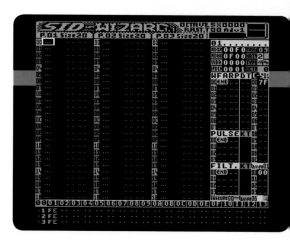

"I had a real synthesizer sound chip, the SID chip. I was beside myself, I had to have one."

Chris Huelsbeck

The SID was designed by a young engineer at MOS Technology named Bob Yannes, an electronic music hobbyist who knew something about music, as well as semiconductors and designing chips he was able to create the MOS Technology 6581 chip, better known as the SID that changed everything.

Yannes later left MOS after the project and started his own company, the well-known electronic musical instrument manufacturer ENSONIQ.

SID (short for Sound Interface Device) is the name of the sound chip used in the C64 and C128.

Bil Herd

I'm from that little window of people that worked for Jack Tramiel and then worked there after Jack Tramiel left. I call this a Commodore Greek tragedy in three acts and I'm from act two, right in the middle of it.

Andy Finkel

Jack's past was known in the company but not in great detail at least not generally. People knew he'd been through a tough time in Germany. He got his start in Toronto and so on but it wasn't a topic of general conversation.

"His experiences in the Second World War were rather horrific"

Leonard Tramiel

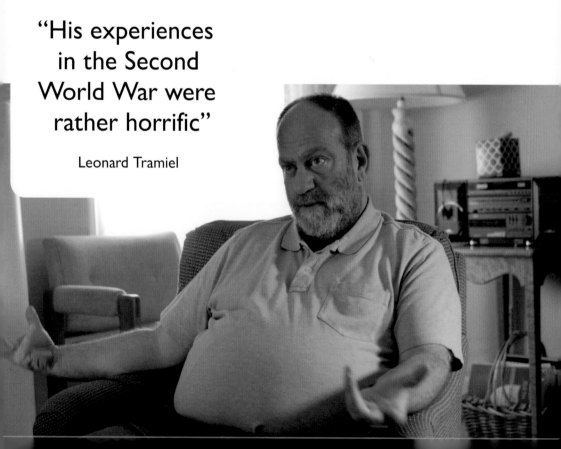

Leonard Tramiel

He often told the story of, I guess it was September 1st 1939 when the Germans invaded Poland. He remembers seeing these squadrons of airplanes flying over, he thought that was really cool and he went outside and saluted it. He didn't think all that highly of them after they came into town.

Lodz was very close to the border in fact so close that they wound up annexing that part of Poland into Germany.

All the Jews were rounded up and sent to live in one particular section of the city called the Ghetto; conveniently not too far from the Jewish cemetery and they were basically slave labour.

I don't actually remember what dad did during the ghetto years but it would have been odd jobs and manual labour of some sort because he was pretty young.

The Lodz ghetto was one of the last if not the last ghetto in Poland to be liquidated and have all its, we'll call them inhabitants, sent to Birkenau, a huge camp part of the Auschwitz complex. Here people were sorted out into those who could work and those that couldn't and those that couldn't were rapidly dispatched.

He wound up going with his dad to a work camp named Ahlem just outside of Hannover.

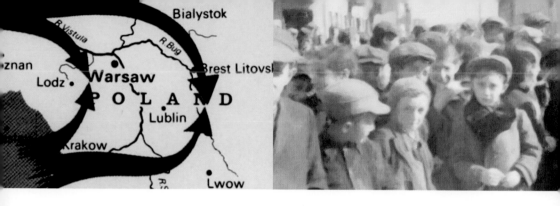

It's funny he said that he remembers trying to never talk about this as we were growing up so as far as he was concerned he never mentioned it. As far as us kids were concerned they talked about it all the damn time and because; and there's nothing inconsistent about that; because there's not a lot of story of that level that a kid can tolerate. Compared to what was bubbling in his mind I'm sure he said nothing.

It was very emotional, really hard to get through but at the end of the war he was deathly ill, too weak to move. So as the Americans were advancing into Germany, the Germans said "OK they're coming in, they're going to kill everyone so if you want to live come with us".

Everyone that could move got up and left, went with the Germans and when they were out of town they were all shot.

Dad told this story that he remembers; which it's almost certainly not true; but he remembers this black American soldier, who he thought was about seven and a half feet tall, come in. He just busted down the door, looked around to see what was going on and quickly got everything going. People in that squadron said there were no blacks. Memory is a funny thing.

Very quickly medical attention was given, the people were taken care of. There were a large number of what were called DPs, or displaced persons camps where people were rejuvenated and allowed to heal and come back to some semblance of their humanity.

My father decided; my parents were married by this point; decided he wanted to come to the US. So the guy asked him "how old are you?" to which my father responded "how old do I need to be?"

He said "eighteen", my father said, "good I'm eighteen".

He was seventeen.

You may find an interesting one-year discrepancy in the year of my father's birth whether it's 1927 or 1928. On all those papers his birth date was 1927 because that made him eighteen at the time, in fact he was born in 1928.

So he arranged to come to the US, joined the US army. My mother also came to the US. He worked in the army mostly because he wanted to learn about the country, learn about the people and wanted to learn English.

5	Thiele	Elsa	64	F	M	German 6 a /	7064 German
6	Tiedeken	Ferdinand	71	M	M	German 6 a /	3805 Ger
7	Tiedeken	Elisabeth	66	F	M	German 6 a /	380 Ger
8	Trojanas	Stasys	35	M	M	Lithuanian 6 e 3	673 Rus
9	Trojanas	Julita	35	F	M	Lithuanian 6 e 3	674 Rus
10	Trojanas	Aukse	3	F	S	Lithuanian 6 d 3	675 Rus
11	Trzmiel	Idek	19	M	S	Polish 6 a 3	495 Po 1
12	Tschetschel	Georg	26	M	M	Stateless 6 e 3	691 Rus
13	Tschetschel	Zofja	26	F	M	Stateless 6 a 3	69 Rus
14	Tsoumalis	Chris	35	M	M	Undetermined 6 e 3	842 Au
15	Tsoumalis	Gertrude	22	F	M	Undetermined 6 a 3	84 Au

You mentioned Ahlem?

A soldier from Sioux Falls, Iowa; if I remember correctly, by the name of Vernon Tott took pictures of the camp that day.

A survivor, who lived across the bay in Oakland, when he retired said "you know I'm going to find these guys" and from memory drew the patch that he remembered on their shoulder and sent it off to the Pentagon and asked what group is this?

He found out, sent a letter to the that squadron and asked does anyone have any memories, any recollection about this?

And Vernon read the the newsletter from his squadron and said, "You know I think I still have those pictures"

So there's a documentary called the 'Angel of Ahlem' about that which is pretty amazing.

We met Vernon in Germany, well I did, my parents had met of course before. There was a ceremony for; I think it was the 60th anniversary of the clearing of the Warsaw, of the Lodz Ghetto. Vernon was in the process of dying of cancer but he came to Germany anyway and participated with us in this. It was really quite moving.

Jack Tramiel (left)

Vernon Tott (right)

'Computer History Museum Silicon Valley 2007'

Interviewer

"Lets focus on 'business is war'"

Jack Tramiel

"Right, don't you want to speak about sex?"

Interviewer

"Maybe later"

Jack Tramiel

"OK"

Leonard Tramiel

My father, for him, business was his life. On the other hand it was very important for him that family be supported and be involved in it. He was quite keen on the idea of his sons working for him.

Michael Tomczyk

I went to see him and I walked into his office. Jack was this short, rotund, bald, swarthy, sort of had large, protruding eyes and a deep booming voice that actually make the walls vibrate it was so baritone. He was very intimidating. He hired me and said,

"Your job will not be to assist me, your job will be to follow me around and learn the religion"

Jack's philosophy of business, he called it the religion.

Leonard Tramiel

I don't know of many other people that could run things quite the way he did. The most surprising thing when you look at the way companies are structured between the lowest level person and the top; there's two or three levels and that's it and no one's that far away. This wound up with an enormous number of people that reported directly to my father.

Leonard Tramiel

There are lots of ways to run a business and if you are going to run a business where the CEO is this warm, gentle, encouraging, mentoring person who leads people through a path of internal and emotional development while they generate a wonderful life changing product – great. I'm sure there are companies that do very well under that model, that wouldn't work with my dad as CEO.

Jack Tramiel (archive footage)

My personal job was not to tell them how good they are but to tell them what they are doing wrong that they can improve.
We live today in a different world.
It's such a good job – my God.

David Pleasance

I went to the CES show, Jack Tramiel was on the stand, he was barking orders to everybody, he was quite aggressive. I had about thirty seconds with him, I just said "hello I'm Dave from the UK" he shook my hand and then dismissed me with his eyes.

Leonard Tramiel

My father was put in touch with a financier in Toronto by the name of Irving Gould who I think at that time got twenty percent of the company.

Very bluntly I asked him one day. I said "Irving I know you're a wealthy man, obviously you invested heavily into Commodore and other companies. Would you mind telling me how you made your money?"

I thought he was just going to throw me out but he didn't, he said "yes I'll tell you".

I'll tell you exactly the words he used.

He said, "David I took the best piss of my life. I'm just stood at the urinal and a young man came in and the young man is going 'so well these guys have invented a system of twenty foot and forty foot containers that can get picked up and carried on lorries and they can get put onto special container ships, cargo ships'

And he said 'and I just brought to my company to the table, to give them the opportunity to have the rights for North America for the containers and they've just turned it down' and Irving just said "you've just found your man".

DAVID PLEASANCE
COMMODORE & AMIGA

THE NEW ATARI

"Jack Attack" is the best arcade-style game yet produced expressly for the popular Commodore 64 system, and rates as an absolute must-b
—Electronic Games Hotline

USE WITH JOYSTICK

Michael Tomczyk

Commodore programmers put together a game called 'Jack attack' and they named it after Jack.

Bil Herd

At Commodore we have something that's sort of an urban legend and yet has its basis in truth and it's called a 'Jack attack'.
'Jack attacks' can actually occur one on one.
Where you you might say, "I just can't work this way you know"
You'd be the president of Commodore and say "I can't work this way" and Jack would say, "Well then don't".
That meant you're fired, you're just out. We lost an entire office one time because they wanted royalties.

Michael Tomczyk

I went to lunch, came back, I looked at the twelve offices and they were all empty. I went up to the receptionist and I said,

"Where's the marketing department?"

She's looking down and writing on a yellow notepad and she said "oh they're gone, Jack came and fired them just before lunch".

Michael worked at Commodore from 1980 to 1984 and was Assistant to Jack and the Marketing Strategist

MICHAEL TOMCZYK
COMMODORE

Leonard Tramiel

The 'Jack attack'. I've know idea where the term came from. The first time I heard it was long after Commodore ceased to be but as I said when my father was 'displeased' he made no secret of it. There were I remember as early as the times I was working in the warehouse that I would be in the warehouse moving pallets around and I could hear dad yelling in his office. I knew someone had not done exactly what he wanted.

Michael Tomczyk

Jack was thought of as being ruthless sometimes because he held you to your word. A young engineering manager once promised to deliver something to him and he wanted six months to do it. So he built up a staff of thirty people and he started working on it.
Six months later to the day Jack showed up and said, "Is it done?"
The engineer said, "no we had some complications, we won't have it done for another six months".
Jack fired everybody and closed down the operation immediately.
Later that afternoon I was in Jack's office when one of the engineers came storming in. He was in his twenties. He said "I've been here for five years, I'm not leaving, I helped build this company, I'm going to sit in the hallway if I have to I'm not being fired".
And Jack said, "fine, go find yourself another job".
And if the twenty-nine other people in that group were smart enough to come and do that they would still have their jobs.

Leonard Tramiel

If he thought you were giving him nonsense he would let you know, usually at fairly high volume levels along with percussion on the nearest horizontal surface. When he was displeased it was obvious.

If you were emotionally resilient enough to handle that and to realize that the criticism was not criticism of you as a person but criticism of the job you had done. You could grow and learn from it, then you wind up with a group of people that will work very well under those circumstances.

LCD

AMIGA

C116

Amiga 500

CD 32

C128

Andy Finkel

My best Jack story happened in Germany.
I had one of the Mercedes for the show and my job was to chauffeur Jack and Sig around. They'd spend a lot of time talking, spend a lot of time touring the show, spend a lot of time in bars. So one time they'd both got really drunk. They were both sitting in the back seat singing German songs; they were having a great time and Jack told the story of how he built this road that we were on because he was a prisoner of war in Germany.

Leonard Tramiel

Everyone talks about him designing all these machines, he neither designed nor actually knew how to use them. The first computer that he was actually comfortable using was an Ipad and when he got comfortable using it he just took to it immediately but he never learned to program, never was interested in doing any of that stuff. He knew it wasn't magic but assumed that if he needed any expertise he would just hire it or he had a son that could do it for him. So it was fine.

ACT 2
COMMODORE FOR
THE MASSES

"My dad brought home, in 1977, a
Commodore PET 2001.
Much like the gamers today that spend all of
their time in their bedrooms that's what I did
with a PET."

Jim Drew

Trevor Dickinson

"My first computer was a Commodore PET 4032."

Commodore
PET

Memory	4-96 KB
CPU Speed	1 MHz
Sound	0
Graphics	2
Rating	9

Phil McCauley

My first experience of computers was the Commodore PET.

The Commodore PET has certain characteristic sounds when you get to know it. First of all there's the sound and the feel of your fingers on the keyboard. A sort of crunching sound, a comforting sound really once you get used to it. Not like keyboards today or anything God forbid flat, glass screens that make no sound, where you have to put a synthesized sound in place. The actual touch from the touch-typing was an important feedback mechanism for the machine.

It was, as I think about quite nostalgically, it was a very comfortable way to type.

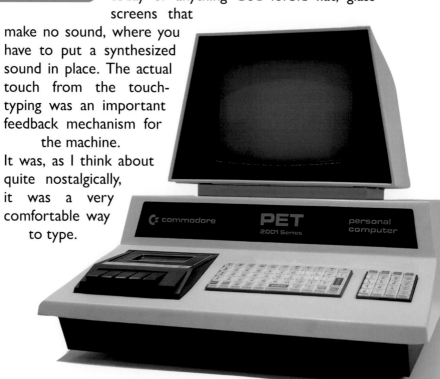

Chuck moved out to California, assembled a small team of people to work on the PET. He did an awful lot of the work himself but there were a few incredibly talented engineers involved, Chuck and me. Chuck knew that it needed to come with a programming language so that you could use it fresh out of the box and the the best one available at the time, to some extent the only one, was Microsoft BASIC.

Gates comes in and says he wants a dollar a machine and my father's response was "I'm already married". So he offered Bill what at the time must have seemed like an enormous amount of money - $50,000, which he took.

Couple of years later Bill is walking around with this entourage of Japanese businessmen and he comes up to the Commodore booth.

If you typed WAIT6502 the next number would be the number of times the word Microsoft was printed on the screen and that's what he expected to happen. Instead the machine just hung there. I leaned over to Bill and said "you know there's nothing at that address, it's just going to hang there" and he gave me the if looks could kill look.

Then I realised what he was doing and said, "Your BASIC has been incredibly important to the to the success of this machine. It's a great product and I'm really glad we have it in our computers" and as a result he let me live.

You may remember the first thing one of these machines would say is COMMODORE BASIC with so many bytes free; so we loaded the program that would read the number of bytes free off of the screen and decode that. If it wasn't the right number it meant that the memory had failed its online power test.

The first model PET had this little or as they called it chiclet keyboard with the little plastic things that came off on your fingers and a cassette tape. The next model had a larger full typewriter spacing keyboard and then you would use an external cassette drive.

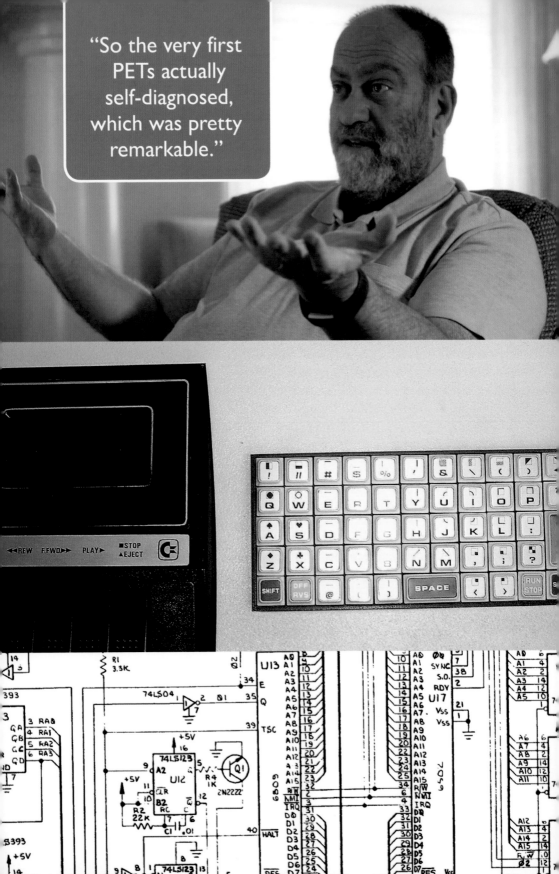

"So the very first PETs actually self-diagnosed, which was pretty remarkable."

My main single contribution to the system was the graphics character set and the only instruction I got from Chuck was four of those images have to be hearts, diamonds, spades and clubs because he wanted to play blackjack.

I think the goal was to have the machine running for the winter CES, Consumer Electronics Show, which didn't work. We eventually figured out what was wrong, there was a resistor missing on the main circuit board otherwise everything worked perfectly but we didn't know that until a couple of weeks later.

So enormous amounts of work went into meeting the deadline of these shows. There was a lot of pressure at that first Hannover fair so I guess that would have been spring of 1977.

It was my job to take the PET. It got its own seat on the airplane next to me, which was lots of fun. Then we had to go through German customs "What do you mean this is a computer? Computers are ten of millions of dollars and they're the size of a room. No it can't be a computer, what are you talking about?"

It went back and forth a couple of times.
In the meantime we had missed the connecting flight from Frankfurt to Hannover. So we rented a VW microbus and drove from Frankfurt to

Hannover, took the PET, popped it down on the table, plugged it in and it didn't work. On the phone we had to diagnose what was going on and repair the machine. Got it working and that was a lot of fun.

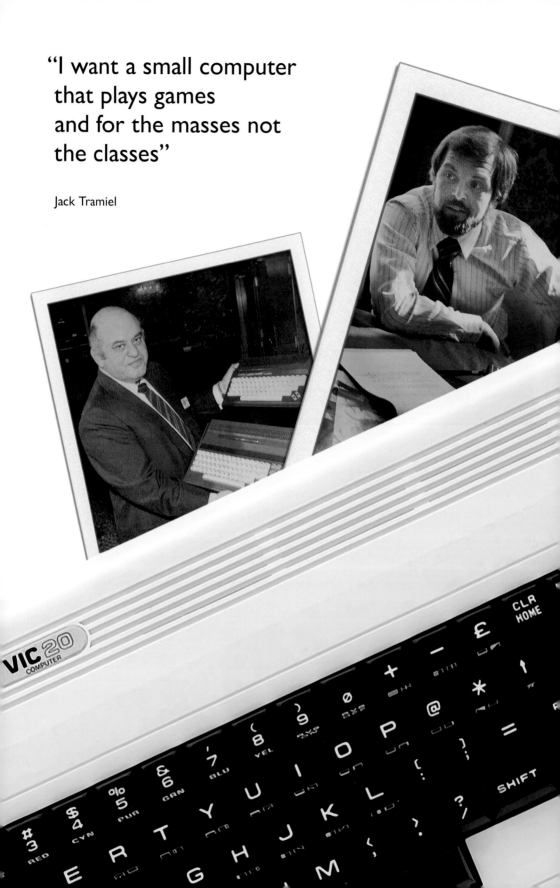

"I want a small computer
that plays games
and for the masses not
the classes"

Jack Tramiel

Warren and Matt

VIC-20 with 8K expansion probably could have got away with it at the time so that was all good.

Fat graphics – yes we like the fat graphics. 20 or 22 characters across?

Yes it was 22. The difference between the VIC and the Commodore's graphics, yes the Commodore was better but sometimes the VIC version is better.

Michael Tomczyk

Commodore was a very international company. We were the third largest personal computer company in the world but we were number three in the US. We were number one in Europe as a result of having sold the Commodore PET computer which was very popular especially in schools.

We were at this meeting and it was a large room with about twenty-five people seated around a square table that was open in the centre. Jack came in and the engineers they wanted to do a colour computer like an Apple and Jack said "I want a small introductory computer, I want a small computer that plays games and for the masses not the classes".

As soon as he said that the whole room erupted and everybody said, "no we have to do a business computer, we have to compete with Apple, we have to do a personal computer, we have to do larger computers not smaller".

Jack said, "I want the small computer but you talk about it and I'll come back tomorrow, I have some business" so he left.

Commodore   C=

VIC-20

Memory   5-40 KB
CPU Speed   1 MHz
Sound   4
Graphics
Rat...

1981

Leonard Tramiel

Dad calls and he says "the engineers have come up with a new machine. I'd like you to come and take a look and see what you think of it".
So I go to Chicago, I go to the the Commodore booth. So there's this little machine in a rectangular box hooked up to a TV showing all sorts of PET graphics, character sets stuff but in colour and that was the birth of the of the VIC-20.

Michael Tomczyk

And that became the first generation of home computers. The first million-seller of home computers that seeded the market.

Andy Finkel

I came on as part of the VIC commando team, which was the VIC-20 product launch team.

Michael Tomczyk

So we launched the VIC-20 at the Consumer Electronics Show in 1981. It was a hit. It actually went on to become the first million-seller home computer; it's the first microcomputer of any kind to sell one million units.

David Murray

When we first got the VIC-20 I had to share it with my brother. It was actually my parents that bought it for me and my brother; he's three years older than me. We didn't have anything else; we just had the computer and the TV. We didn't have any games for it, we didn't have any software for it, all we had was the computer and the manual.
So we started playing around trying to figure out how to program in BASIC. They had some example programs in the manual and it would teach you how to do things. Then once I learned that I started making my own programs.

```
**** CBM BASIC V2 *
3583 BYTES FREE
READY.
```

Warren and Mat

The fat graphics really added to some
of the shooters. They were just chunky
but fun.
Yes and the sort of sound effects were
just sort of raucous.
Well you're firing everything out the
sound chip.
Why isn't it blowing up?

But it was
that good.
The sound's massively loud through the
speakers thinking is this real?

Commodore   **C=**

VIC1001

Memory	5-40 KB
CPU Speed	1 MHz
Sound	4
Graphics	4
Rating	7

Is this going to really happen?
But that was how it was, it got your
attention.
Some massive overly loud zapping
sound, that'll draw you straight in.
'Ooh playing this then'.
You would always have to be wary of the fact of 'oh can this game
run on unexpanded VIC or do I need 8K or 16K expansion?'
Thankfully a lot of games companies realised that you didn't want
to take a chance with the game and realise it doesn't work so they'd
always put 'Unexpanded VIC-20' in nice, big, bold letters on the
cover.

Michael Tomczyk

The VIC could be programmed but it only had 5K of RAM memory. When you turned it on the 5K shrunk down to 3.5K. 3.5K is basically one sheet of typing papers worth of memory. Today we have gigabytes.

Andy Finkel

We wired up the memory externally to the VIC-20 and that gave us a full 8K of RAM to develop cartridges in. Once we got that we could actually start developing more significant cartridges, more complicated games like Omega Race, Gorf, Sargon II Chess, the adventure games and things like that. Couldn't do those on 3.5K but 8K was barely enough.

David Murray

"Some of our family members gave us some Christmas presents that were VIC-20 cartridge games. We got Omega Race, some kind of Sea Battle or something like that. Omega Race was definitely the best one. I still have that cartridge."

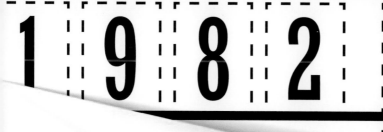

Commodore	
C64	
Memory	64 KB
CPU Speed	1 MHz
Sound	8
	7

Leonard Tramiel

The real winner of course was the Commodore 64, which was the natural outgrowth of the VIC. The same people that designed that VIC chip designed the VIC-II, which is what powered the Commodore 64 and then it had an absolute brilliant sound chip.

Kenny McAlpine

The Commodore with it's Sound Interface Device or the SID chip, as it's affectionately known, really bundled up a hardware synthesizer inside a home computer. I knew then that that was a computer that I just had to get my hands on.

Rob Hubbard

A lot of the music on the games at that time in the very early eighties was just really awful.

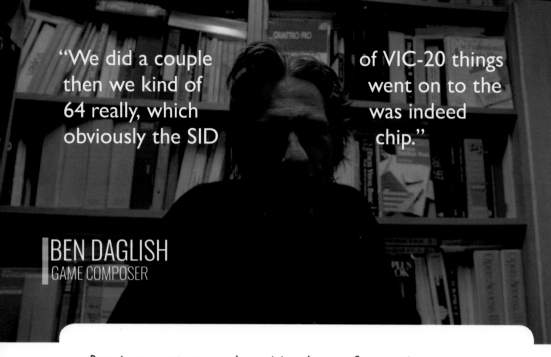

BEN DAGLISH
GAME COMPOSER

Ben is a composer and musician known for creating many game soundtracks for the Commodore 64.

Rob Hubbard

I just had to choose the C64 because of the 64K memory and the fact that it had a sound chip where none of the others did.

Ben Daglish

Hearing a piece of Rob's I think it was his arrangement of English Country Gardens, was it for Hover Bovver or something like that?
You know yum de da dum da da dum but it's a lovely arrangement and had some lovely little sounds, little twiddles in it.

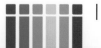

"The Commodore 64 sound chip. It was a decade ahead of everything else"

MIKE CLARK
GAME COMPOSER

Mike Clark

The Commodore 64 sound chip. It was a decade ahead of everything else. So even to the stage of where the Amiga came out the Amiga couldn't do the sounds that the Commodore 64 was doing. It was that good.

Elektron created The Sidstation based on the legendary MOS6581 SID chip. This gritty sounding synthesizer is the reason why Elektron as a company was formed in the first place.

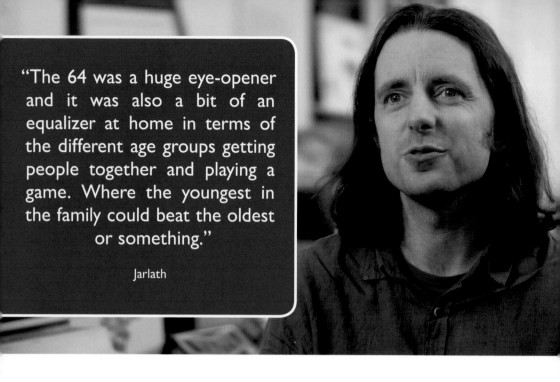

"The 64 was a huge eye-opener and it was also a bit of an equalizer at home in terms of the different age groups getting people together and playing a game. Where the youngest in the family could beat the oldest or something."

Jarlath

Andrew Fisher

I've been a Commodore 64 fan since 1985 and in that time I've been involved in programming, composing music, running a disc magazine and have also written a book about Commodore 64 games.

"I've been a Commodore 64 fan since 1985"

ANDREW FISHER
RETRO GAMER WRITER

Serafin Fuente

There was no Internet at the time. There was no easy way, even getting to the library was difficult. It was hard for your parents to haul five kids to the library but there were these gems of resources that we would find just on trips to the grocery store.

I knew there was a big store that was nearby, I'd bring a pad and paper and actually write the machine code myself, copying it because I couldn't buy the book. So I would sit there while my mom was shopping or while she was doing her thing. I would come home and have a piece of it, bring it to my Commodore 64 and have that stored and I would have to wait another week to go by to get that next little piece.

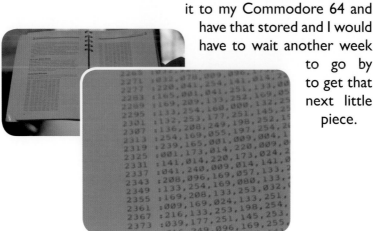

Mark Knight

First Commodore 64 for I think three to fours years and bearing in mind it was second-hand anyway but it got to the point where it would only load games if the cassette deck was upside down. Sometimes I had to bang the computer on the desk to get it to work. I guess I was seating the chips back in their sockets but as a twelve/thirteen year old I had no idea about that sort of thing.

Dan Wood

Commodore 64 was an amazing machine. My best friend Shaun at school, he had a Commodore 64 and I was sort of envious because it was actually one of the newer ones that came out. It was the little sleek-looking white ones.

Joe Blade was a brilliant game on the Commodore 64. It was actually set in like the far distant future in the year 1997 when London had been taken over by thugs. We got really far in that game and I remember we actually left this Commodore 64 on for about a week because we didn't want to lose our high score.

DAN WOOD
THE RETRO HOUR

Kenny McAlpine

When I got the Commodore the technology of the sound chip meant that I could explore musical ideas that perhaps lay just beyond my technical playing ability. I was really, really into Ragtime for example and I heard a couple of Ragtime-y kind of tracks in Rob Hubbard's soundtrack to Action Biker and then Martin Galway's soundtrack to Kong Strikes Back. That was the point really when I realised that the Commodore 64 could be a vehicle for exploring composition and performance in a way that didn't necessarily rely on instrumental technique.

Anthony Clarke

I love music and we wanted to do something different with music. I remember seeing this advertisement in one of the computer magazines from this guy Rob Hubbard that basically said 'I'll write music for your games' and I think he even posted us a cassette to say 'here's some of the stuff I've done'.

Rob Hubbard

Eventually it clicked as to how it worked and what it was actually doing. Then once you get that stuff working without the computer crashing then basically it was like Pandora's box opening up. I was thinking much more about the about the SID chip.

Dan Wood

It kind of became like a popularity contest really the more games you had the cooler you were at school. If you were that kid that would come in with that new game that had just come out in the shop on Monday morning that every kid in school was asking for you'd be the most popular kid in school that week.

Vassilis Pateras

Commodore gaming was promoted through the use of clubs.

Whoever had the faster ability of doing...tap, tap, tap, click... or click, click, click... or this - would obviously be the winner. Whoever got the most points we used to buy prizes as opposed to sweets, obviously the Greek element would be buying a pile of souvlaki.

Andrew Fisher

At school there were lots of people with different machines. I had a friend who had a Spectrum and I had friends who had the Commodore 64 as well and we would occasionally swap games to try something out. I remember one lunch time running home from school with Ghostbusters, the tie in to the film and playing that for about half an hour instead of having lunch.

Rob Hubbard

There was a really awful sample that was used on the Ghostbusters game. It became apparent that you could do samples. What I wanted to do was try to find a way to be able to play a sample not just a little speech sample with nothing else going on but to get something integrated in the music, so distorted rock guitar was an obvious choice.

Chris has written soundtracks for more than 70 games, many of them Commodore 4 titles, including the urrican series.

Chris Huelsbeck

What could I do with the technology to get more out of the sound chips? One of the things that I developed was sampling. I realised you can play the SID voices, the three voices whilst the sampling plays over it. That was a revelation and they did it with the volume register.

CHRIS HUELSBECK
COMMODORE & AMIGA

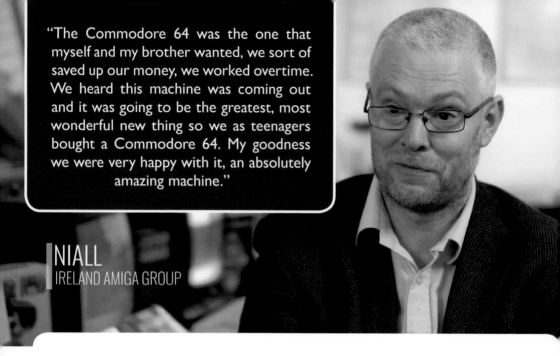

"The Commodore 64 was the one that myself and my brother wanted, we sort of saved up our money, we worked overtime. We heard this machine was coming out and it was going to be the greatest, most wonderful new thing so we as teenagers bought a Commodore 64. My goodness we were very happy with it, an absolutely amazing machine."

NIALL
IRELAND AMIGA GROUP

Dan Wood

What was the culture like at Commodore UK? Was was it hard work? Was it a lot of partying? What went on?

"There was always partying. We really I guess supported the idea that 'you work hard, you play hard'."

David Pleasance

Gail Wellington

Soon as David joined, I met David Pleasance when he first joined the company in sales. I was already there and David was a master of creating interesting bundles for retail.
Great, great program that was developed while I was there was International Soccer.

Trevor Dickinson

I walked past a computer store and I saw a game playing in the window and it was International Soccer on the Commodore 64. There was colour, there was sound, there was animation, there were graphics. I just had to have that machine.

Gail Wellington

This game was unbelievable and it was only possible because the 64 had sprites. No other computer had these programmable, movable objects.

Simon Mattisson

So the SID station was a project at Chalmers University of Technology where a couple of guys had this course to make something that involved programmable logic. They had two ideas; one was a MIDI CD converter and the other was something called SIDomania.
SIDomania was a synthesizer based on the SID chip. The SID station is a tabletop synthesizer module. It's got a few direct controls that control sound parameters.

It's got a few things for entering tables and stuff that you would do on a on a regular Commodore 64 and a tracker but in a hardware box.

SIMON MATTISSON
ELEKTRON SWEDEN

Bil Herd

Hey, there's this company called Commodore hiring.
Yes I need to get out of here.
So without really knowing; I was saving my money for an
Atari 400, I couldn't even afford an 800 back then. I didn't
know much about Commodore and I was about to become
an Atari fan but that stopped the day I got to Commodore.

Hedley Davis

We brought this Commodore 64 and it was totally amazing
because we had a PDP 23 I think it was. The boss was very
    "Oh you have to be very careful around the PDP 23"
And here's Bil with this Commodore 64 and you can type in
'LOAD, $8, 8' or whatever but it would do a disc drive
in a directory and all these things. So I was like
'working on computers seems a little
bit more interesting than
    building scales'.

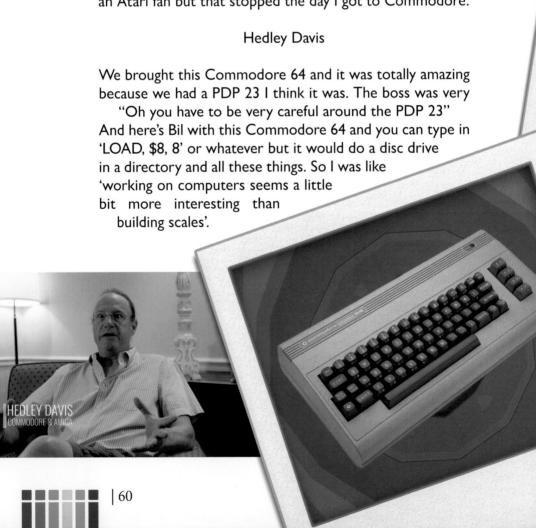

I go to interview with Bob Russell who worked on parts of the VIC-20 and C64. It's going OK and stuff but then at one point he said "why am I LOADX immediate 02?" and I'd go "8502"

He looks at me and he goes "then I'd store immediate" and I'm like "8D109"

I'm muttering the opcodes that I know from having worked on the 6502 so closely.

I saw his body language change.

He's like "Ok we'll have you down to the plant type thing".

Well he phrased it so nonchalantly, just swing by the plant. I thought I was going for burgers or something. I don't even bring my resume and I'm in corduroys or something when I swing by.

The first thing I do is when I go to interview with Shiraz Shivji, who's the guy who's either going to hire me or not. He had his desk turned around the wrong way and I didn't know so I walk in and pop myself in his chair.

He walks in and has to say "excuse me, you are in my chair".

He then goes "where's your resume?"

I'm going "I didn't bring one!"

I think the interview is over at that point but now Frank Hughes stops by and he goes "Oh Shiraz I got it".

He brings it in and I'm starting to kind of hit my stride, talking and stuff. I just happen to mention K-Tron the vibrating wire technology, I know it's one of our competitors but I went into the detail. If you say you're a satellite, you better be able to talk satellite.

Well I'm weighing instrumentation so I better talk it. "So what I did there was' I said, "it uses a reference weight versus a regular weight and it can even work on the moon" Shiraz looked at me and said "you meant mass" and I was hired because he got to correct me.

I was early enough when I joined Commodore that we were still up in the MOS building.

So it's these tiny rooms painted psychotic blue and there were three engineers in there and if you didn't need the door you could've put a fourth engineer in there. None of us cared because there's a chip fabricator right below our feet.

So that's where I did what became known as the TED series of computers. I did that while working at the MOS building. Then after we moved down to Westchester into that huge facility there, we got Hedley and a guy named Terry Fisher 'Fish' who joined us and he did all the PC boards. The cream of the crop of the skill company was now down here.

Hedley Davis

One of the very first tasks I was given came from a guy named Andy Finkel. He told me to re-write the cassette loader code for the C128 to make it run faster and run better than the code that was used on the C64 but he put this one perverse constraint 'you cannot move any labels'. So every label in the assembly code had to stay in exactly the same place because Andy was of the opinion that programmers would randomly jump to any label that had got out there and they were all public. So it was a very odd thing to have to do but that's what I ended up doing.

Dave Haynie

The John Lennon looking guy was there and that was Bil Herd. He proceeded to ask me some technical questions about saturation limiting diodes on the input of op amps and also about Laplace transforms, which he didn't know how to do. I think we had a really good interview and sure enough a day or so later they called me in to visit Commodore on Monday and offered me a job on the spot.

Bil Herd

I had the long hair going so I looked like Floyd the drummer of the Muppet Show, the way he walked. I was unlike most people because in California I might have been more normal but out here on the East coast our engineers had actually turned into a pretty stodgy bunch and I was able to help turn it back into animal house. Then we had fun.

Hedley Davis

A guy I used to work with was a guy named George Robbins.
He was a character.
I say we lived at Commodore, we worked at Commodore,
we would go home at night and at least sleep in our bed,
occasionally take as shower and show up the next day.
George lived at work. George had two cubicles where the
rest of us had one. George had a nest.

Dave Haynie

"George had managed to get caught once driving a car with no driver's licence, an expired registration and no insurance."

George Robbins (archive footage)

I parked the truck against a telephone pole
After the cops were done with me and I'd like take care of a
little detail like call Hedley
So he gave me a ride into Commodore you know not long
after I became known as the resident Commodore person.

Dave Haynie

So George just decided he was going to live at Commodore. Greg Berlin and I had discovered that down in the factory area up in this weird sort of mid-floor area in the factory was a place where they would stash all the Herman Miller furniture. To improve our offices we would put up doorways and things that weren't ever supposed to be there. George had done the same thing only even more so that he had made himself a little room that he could close off, which we called his nest.

Bil Herd

Yes I was the one who coined the phrase 'nesting'. Whereas I had the air mattress and stuff George would sleep in bubble wrap. He'd get up and he'd be walking around and he'd have these red rings, blinking his eyes and stuff but he'd have these little impressions all over his face from the bubble wrap.
When you went to look for George, because he didn't always sleep in the same place, you'd look under something see like a foot sticking out of bubble wrap – found him! It was literally like a mouse nest at that part, so we called it nesting.

Dave Haynie

I kept a sleeping bag. I could sleep under my desk when I needed to but I wasn't planning to live there full-time but George kind of was. He'd also take sponge baths in the bathroom. We didn't have a shower. He was kind of a character and that's just part of it.
George got paid in cash, he didn't have direct deposit and at some point they found out that he had six months of uncashed pay cheques in his drawer, in his office because he was never leaving. Maybe to eat he'd drive, all of us would, we had cars and we'd go out.

Hedley Davis

We are all in our twenties and thirties and we're getting paid good money we think we're doing okay. So George has decided he needs money and he reaches into his pocket and he pulls out six months worth of pay cheques.
"What's that George?"
He said, "Oh I need to cash some out" because he needs a deposit. He didn't spend any money, he didn't have any expenses, he lived in the building. He had this huge pile.
He filled out six months of pay cheques and of course I'm sitting there going "oh man what I could do with that". We are all "wow that's a, that's a chunk of change".

Dave Haynie

He was forced by personnel to open an account with direct deposit because I guess they didn't like the idea of cheques not being cashed.
Yes it was funny, you could you could come up with a lot of different George stories if you thought about it.

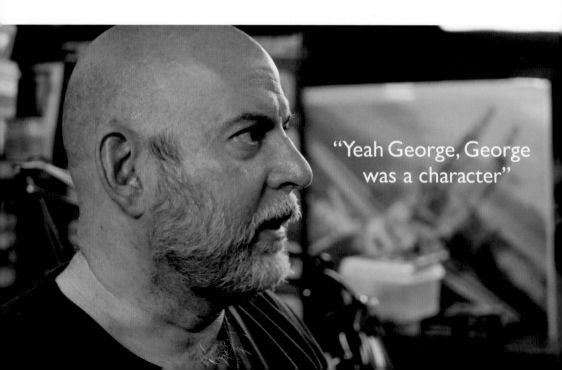

"Yeah George, George was a character"

Hedley Davis

We worked to go to CES and George was an engineer, a key engineer on the product, actually it might have been when the A500 came out and the mandate came down that everybody going to CES had to wear a suit. So you had to have a tie and a suit and you had to look good.

All of George's attire were blue jeans with battery acid holes in them and ripped T-shirts just because he didn't feel that dressing up was sort of his thing but he wanted to go to CES and so he needed to get a suit. So he goes out and he buys this synthetic material, polyester suit, sort of tan coloured and he's got the suit. We are in the labs and we have to figure out how to get to CES. The rest of us have this thing called luggage that we put our clothes in but George doesn't possess any of this so he's not sure exactly what he's going to do. So literally he takes a grocery bag and he jams his suit in the grocery bag. He rolls the grocery bag over and he puts duct tape on the outside of the bag and this is his luggage.

So he takes this thing and I'll never forget sitting there in Las Vegas waiting for the luggage to come down and here comes George's bag rolling down.

So then what happened?

Well it's a polyester suit and it's been all scrunched up and compressed. He puts the suit on and now the sleeves are up to here and he's got this wrinkly suit on. He shows up and management finally said "George you don't have to work the booth, you don't have to wear the suit, go see CES" and they never really fought him on that again.

One of the best engineers I ever worked with.

"It took a few years to get around this and now I have my own car and my own house and I don't live at Commodore anymore but I love it anyway."

George Robbins

Michael Tomczyk

Commodore stock went through the ceiling, the Commodore stock went up and split a couple of times. In fact Jack and his three sons had a tradition that whenever the stock went up ten points they would all stop and share a bottle of Dom Perignon champagne.

I'm privileged to say I was with them several times when they did that. That was pretty cool and it's an interesting symbol of the growth we were achieving.

We were not just growing the market. We weren't just giving millions of people a computer that they couldn't afford before. We were also making a lot of money for investors and showing that this was a profitable enterprise.

Commodore
C64

Memory	
CPU Speed	64 KB
Sound	1 MHz
Graphics	8
Rating	7
	10

Apple
II

Memory	
CPU Speed	6
Sound	6
Graphics	
Rating	

Bil Herd

Jack Tramiel did his Apple killer and it was the Commodore 64. He was done with Apple. We used to say Apple who? I mean they were cooked in our book.

It's true we did twenty-seven million C64's where as Apple 2 might have sold five and a half million or something.

So we didn't need another games machine what Jack wanted was Sir Clive Sinclair's spot now. He had the little Spectrum and things and he wanted him next.

The C116 it was this big; it was the Raspberry Pi of the day. It was supposed to cost $49, it had chiclet keys but it had 121 colours, had built in sound, all in one chips, basically it was a chip with a computer built around it.

Back then it used to be lots of chips.

Leonard Tramiel

As the company got more and more successful and more and more perks came up like, as my father called it, the PET jet. Although it probably should have been called the Commodore 64 jet but that didn't sound as good.

Irving would demand use of the PET jet whenever he could and dad didn't like this, it did not fit with his morals of what the right thing for a company asset to be used for.

Commodore Cᴇ
C116

Memory	16 KB
CPU Speed	1.76 Mhz
	5
	6

Bil Herd

Then there was the one with the full size keyboard and TED meant text display. It was supposed to be a business machine. You want to play games get a 64.
In a matter of fact the price is completely different but we're not trying to compete with ourselves.
So Jack had that focus that he knew what he wanted to do with the market.

Leonard Tramiel

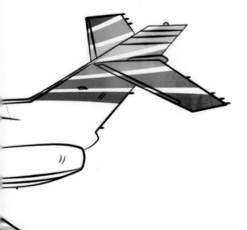

I think both Commodore and Apple had in 1983, so the CES was in January of 1984, had just each cost a billions dollars in annual sales. As I like to point out Commodore doing it with machines that cost a tenth as much as the Apple machines. So a few more machines being sold.

FOR $595, YOU GET WHAT NOBODY ELSE CAN GIVE YOU FOR TWICE THE PRICE.

Andy Finkel

An argument going on between Jack and Irving upstairs in the booth and I was there demonstrating and suddenly somebody came over and said you have to come up and explain the plus/4 to them. So I went up, I didn't really know Irving I know Jack a lot better and so I went through my spiel explaining what it was, what we wanted it to do, how it was going to prop up the price of the C64. The people in the room listened and then I was dismissed.

Leonard Tramiel

There was a celebration for Commodore's; I guess it was 25th anniversary at the time or the 30th, if I do the math quickly.
Dad gave Irving an ultimatum and said, "You can't use company assets as if they're your own, as long as I'm president you can't, you have to stop. So either you stop doing it or I quit". To which Irving said "goodbye" and dad quit. Just left the room and quit. Walked by my wife in the hall and looking rather stern and upset. She was kind of shocked and that's it he just quit.

There are all sorts of stories. I think the official Commodore story is that there was a board meeting in New York a couple of weeks later where they fired him. I'm pretty sure he wasn't at the meeting.

"When Jack leaves, and he leaves literally at a CES, Jack has a disagreement with Irving Gould, they part ways literally at the CES show and at that point TED literally died because now there is nobody to focus all those things."

Bil Herd

The new generation Corvettes. So the three of us got together and bought him one of these Corvettes at that same Consumer Electronics Show. So Sam and Garry drove it down to Las Vegas for that same show and unbeknownst to us that this whole quitting Commodore thing was going to happen we were going to give him this fun present.

So Garry arranges to have the car parked in the front of the hotel and then they went outside on some pretence. Dad walks out and sees the car and goes "that's it, that's the car, that's what I want". He walks up to it and he goes "it's the right colour and it's got all the right wheels and the right interior and the right everything and this is perfect".

So Garry reaches into his pocket, pulls out the keys and says, "it's yours".

1984 CORVETTE

"Then a couple of days later he quits and hops in the car and drives home."

Dave Haynie

I didn't really know him, I'd seen him a couple of times but Jack was still there, he didn't leave until after Consumer Electronics Show that January.

A couple of weeks after that is when he left so yes I was there basically for the tail end of the Jack Tramiel era. It didn't really have an impact. A lot of the people who had made the Commodore 64 had left a long time ago.

Bil Herd

Without Jack around the sheep started multiplying without a wolf and pretty soon we're stepping in sheep shit everywhere. Meanwhile we go from a core of about eight to twelve people doing all the work, the department blooms up to fifteen and it's still the same core of eight to twelve of us doing all the work.

They didn't know the new computer you have to start over again. Get developers on board. This is more than marketing that dropped the ball. Anybody that had only been there a couple of years thought that C64's sell themselves. They sure acted like they did we sold 27 million of them. But then they upped the price for the TED series and called it the Plus/4 it became $300, it was designed to be $79.

So that thing now dies on the vine but what that shows then is with Jack we had a focus.

He didn't think a distributor should make any money off hardware and he didn't think we should make too much money off hardware. He thinks you should have a good price 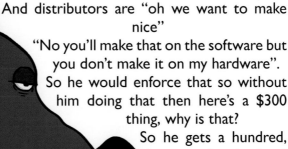 for a good product but not overcharge.

And distributors are "oh we want to make nice"

"No you'll make that on the software but you don't make it on my hardware".

So he would enforce that so without him doing that then here's a $300 thing, why is that?

So he gets a hundred, he gets a hundred and he gets a hundred.

Michael Tomczyk

Fifty top executives, engineers and marketeers at Commodore all walked out of the company in one week. It's as if we set our time clock six months, we never talked to each other. The six-month point came, we weren't happy with what we saw at the company.
We weren't being allowed to develop the new computers that we had in mind. We had a lot of new stuff and prototypes in development, so we all walked out. Greg Pratt the president of Commodore USA, me, all the VIC Commandos, many of the engineers, the whole infrastructure just walked out in one week.

Commodore	
C128	
Memory	128 KB
CPU Speed	4 MHz
Sound	8
	7

Bil Herd

I jumped ship to what had been called the D128 and there's a story with the day that happened. We ended up in engineering deciding to do the C128 because no one stopped us.

This wasn't from on high, this wasn't "there's our project to plan for this year".

With a couple of engineers I sat down at a table, I threw away the old guy's design because it just wasn't going to go anywhere, used their little grid paper and hand drew a schematic that became the C128.

We show it to management when we'd get a certain distance and they're like "this is great, I had a great idea" we're like "I need another guy on my team" replies "yes you've got it".

So we marched it down field by building up resources and things but we told them it's now called the C128, it was us that decided to make it Commodore compatible to the Commodore 64.

We hadn't said a hundred percent compatible, that was marketing once again drifting through the picture like they were in a drunken haze "oh it's a hundred percent compatible" well no, we never said that but we'll try.

Dave Haynie

"Yes it's hard to say, I think a lot of people just like the idea it's bigger, better, faster, more but is also runs my old programs so I don't have to keep the Commodore 64 around, which is a significant thing."

Bil Herd

The 128 was there to fill a gap. We needed something for CES and we know the Amiga's coming. I'm actually one of the people they brought in and I looked at the spec and said, "Why are there tanks instead of business icons?".
We saw the 128 as just basically 'if the main thrust of the allied forces was the Amiga it was me and my crew that went up to the mountains and held the mountain pass for the winter' that's how I look at it. And so the 128 was only meant to sell one year.

Dave Haynie

I know we sold six or seven million of them at least and it worked more than most companies were selling as far as a single model of the computer. It didn't match the twenty-something million of the C64 but nobody else did either.

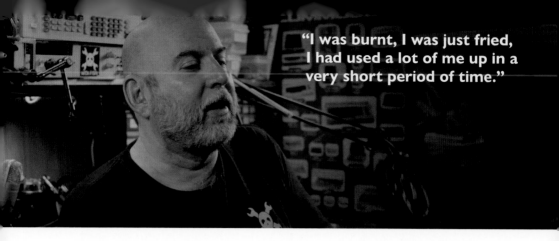

"I was burnt, I was just fried, I had used a lot of me up in a very short period of time."

There was supposed to a C128D and that was my favourite computer. It was supposed to come out at the exact same time. It's the one with the built-in drive, the keyboard clipped under it and it didn't get made. I didn't know it didn't get produced until after I'd quit because I kind of wandered off after, I was burnt, I was just fried, I had used a lot of me up in a very short period of time.

"Do you know the hole-in-the-wall story?"

"Have you heard the hole-in-the-wall story?"

Bil Herd

Ok, so the hole-in-the-wall story.

We, as you know, we were working very hard and didn't need delays that we didn't need to be there in the first place and Commodore found a new way to throw one in front of us. I'd moved into this one room where I had this big emulator and on the weekends they would turn off the air conditioner. So I would wear a headband and no shirt and I would have to keep washing it off about every twenty minutes with spray because I'd dripped sweat on it. None the less it was my room and that's where I did my work.

Then one day I show up and the door's locked on the weekend. "Oh this is inconvenient".

So I climb up over the ceiling and I get that white crap all over me and I open the door and we put up a sign that says 'don't lock this door, there is no key for it' because it was a brand new facility for us and they'd never ever turned the key over we figured.

Well the security guards can't resist a door than can be locked and locked it again.

Climb up over, get the white crap all over me again, put a sign that says 'no don't lock this door, there's no key for it'. I may have said assholes or something.

So finally it's locked again.

They said I could punch through the wall in one punch. It was actually two, one for the inside layer, one for the outside layer to where I could reach in and unlock the door.

So by the time I've got it open I've got the white crap all over my arm now instead of me and there's a bunch of Z8000 programmers looking like I just shot a sheep or something and the next day they locked the door again.

So I had to put a sign up that said 'look assholes there's a f****ing hole in the wall, stop locking the door'.

That's the hole-in-the-wall story.

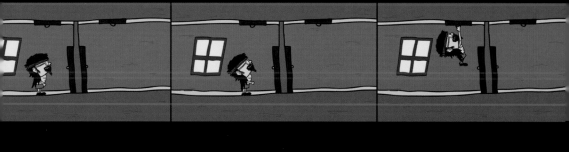

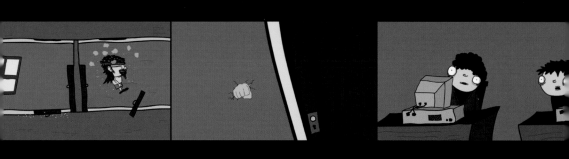

ACT 3
RISE OF THE AMIGA

1984 to 1986, Robert J. Mical worked for Amiga Corporation and then Commodore International.

"You don't get to bark. We're doing something important here where no barking is important. Are we rolling?"

RJ Mical

Welcome to RJ Mical's house of construction, ha-ha ha-ha. You know you probably won't be able to get to shown any of the house, will you?

Crew

Don't worry I can see it right now!

RJ Mical

Yes, oh good, ok well.

I'm RJ Mical and I was one of the original engineers that invented the Amiga computer a long time ago and since then I've done a lot with my life. I've done a lot with my career and managed to go a lot of places. But I've got to tell you that the Amiga thing stands out as one of the most precious and special periods of my life and I think the thing I've created that I'm most delighted about.

"When I first got into Amiga I was a very young kid and this was a fantastic escape and that machine I absolutely loved."

RAVI ABBOTT
THE RETRO HOUR

"The sound on the Amiga was a bit of a game changer so for the first time video game music and computer music began to sound like production music."

Kenny McAlpine

"When I saw the specs of the Amiga and some demos and stuff like that I was like 'this is the next level'."

CHRIS HUELSBECK
COMMODORE & AMIGA

"My love is the Amiga 500 and the CD32."

PAUL BRIDGER
CD32 & AMIGA ENTHUSIAST

"I got an Amiga 1000 and I was probably mostly known for doing the Budbrain mega demos 1 and 2."
Kim Frederiksen

KIM FREDERIKSEN
BUDBRAIN DEMO

Denmark

Kenny

The first time I played the Amiga was when my cousin had it. My cousin was four years older than me so he had this Amiga and we were going up to his house and there was just this magic.

RJ Mical

I'm at the University of Illinois and I'm an English major. I'm studying to get an English degree, not sure exactly what I'm going to do with it, literature maybe, writing for newspapers or magazines or something like that. But I didn't want to do literature; I didn't want to write for magazines. I wanted to write books; I wanted to do my own creation.
But I was afraid of being a starving artist and then I was going to go out into the real world and be unable to be really successful and have a great income and so on.
All the things I'd been taught that I really wanted which turned out to be not true but I was scared to go out and get out into the real world with an English degree.
I had this amazing fateful afternoon that I'm sitting in the computer lab and I'm about to graduate and I'm worried what am I going to do out there in the real world with an English language degree?
And I'm sitting there in the computer lab worrying what am I going to do? What am I going to do? And then I take a break from my worrying to play some of my computer game; the Star Trek game that I played. So I play the game for a while, then I'd stop and worry what am I going to do with my life? What am I going to do with my life?
Then I'd play the game and I'd worry what am I going to do with my life? And finally hey I know: I could do this stuff. I realised all of an instant in one afternoon that really my calling was to go off and to do software engineering.

In roughly December of 1982 Dave Morris convinced me that I should come work with him at Initial Amiga, actually it was still Hi-Toro at the time; it was named Amiga I think a few months after I got there. When I got there I was the first technical employee of any kind there. Dave had eight other marketing and sales people working on the game controller and other things to prep the channel.

Jay Miner officially couldn't be there because part of the deal was that he would stay at ZyMOS and finish the pacemaker. So I arrived there by myself and then later on Jay and Joe Decuir would stop by and the team of the three of us were given a room with three very large wall-sized whiteboards to come up with a product.

Ron Nicholson

RJ Mical

Not only was working at Williams Electronics an amazing experience because it gave me this opportunity to really express myself as a computer scientist but also as an artist. I'm a storyteller; I love creating music; I love creating graphics and special effects and it was a job that allowed me to tie all of that together and do something. But even better than that I met a fellow there that got connected shortly after that with this new company out in California called Amiga Computer.

Ron Nicholson

Dave Morris basically told us what the channel was and what he wanted to put in the channel and we were given pretty much a clean slate to do it. He wanted something that could produce animation more like the cartoons kids saw on TV. So we started on the whiteboard just drawing boxes and one of us would throw up an idea and you know Jay would shake his head and say "no feasible".
Of course the fourth person in the room was Mitchy Jay's dog who would actually sit there watching. The stories are that we would look at Mitchy and Mitchy would either nod or fall asleep and we would use that as a cue to the design.

RJ Mical

The original Amiga that I saw in the block diagram had game controller ports as part of its design and all of that it checked out as a proper game system but it also had these extra capabilities. It was that more than anything else that inspired me to join the company because the games stuff was interesting to me and to create a game platform I probably would have said yes if it was just that.

Ron Nicholson

The Amiga is sort of the child of Commodore and Apple and Atari. Jay and Joe Decuir had worked on Atari and of course they knew about the sprite engines that were in the Atari VCS. The chips they had worked with were the 6502, which had come from Commodore of course; Chuck Peddle's chip. Then I had worked at Apple and learned the tricks that Woz and Burrell Smith used in the Apple 2 and the Mackintosh and of course the work that Lisa had reinvented from the Xerox Alto.
So we sort of combined ideas from that whole ecosystem of computers that had come before and I think that was one of the reasons the Amiga turned out so well, the cross-pollination of ideas from multiple predecessor designs.

RJ Mical

What I saw more than anything else was the quality, the strength of the people that were putting together the company. The engineering staff was superb and I was easily convinced by people like Dale Luck and Ron Nicholson and of course Jay Miner.

The business people really believed and were extremely well experienced and had the right know how, the right enthusiasm to be able to make the thing happen and so I said yes to joining Amiga Computer.

Ron van Schaik

I am the chairman of the Dutch Commodore User Group. Our club is more than 35 years old and still alive and kicking.

Arn

I like to collect old computers mainly Commodores.

Ron van Schaik

We have almost four hundred members. Our club meetings are visited by about fifty to a hundred visitors every time and six times a year we are here in Maarssen in the Netherlands. It's a very nice place to be because we have a lot to do with innovation.

Ron Nicholson

Somehow Dave Needle got introduced to us as a consultant who possibly could help with some of the general hardware design, logic design and chip design. He came to an interview, actually they didn't like him at the first interview and sent him away.
He sort of begged his way back in basically because he had seen the whiteboard and decided that whiteboard was better than anything else that he'd seen to work on.

RJ Mical

When I joined Amiga I originally joined with the graphics staff, there's a fellow named Dale Luck who was in charge of the graphics development for the Amiga and I joined to work for him and to work on graphics. It worked out well. But as time went on and as the company continued to grow and to develop I ended up taking on more and more responsibilities for running the team with my boss at the time.

Ron Nicholson

The technology these days is to put billions of transistors on a chip, a few decades ago it was millions. Back when we were designing the Amiga putting several thousand transistors on a chip was a very difficult task. In retrospect we were trying to do a project that was nearly impossible for the team size that we had.

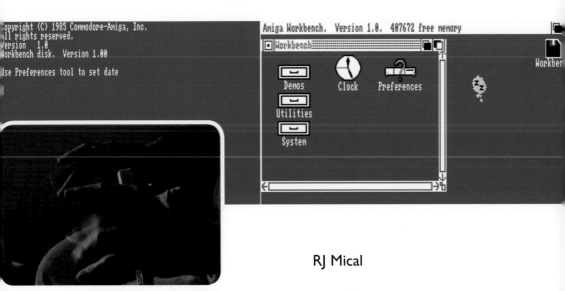

RJ Mical

All computers at that point were switching to being user interface oriented. It was no longer good enough to have a computer where the user had to type cryptic text into a text window and command the computer to do things by knowing the right instructions to give. The new world was one where it was a graphical user interface and you interacted with it with your hands and it was a much more rich and enriching sort of environment that needed to be created. The Amiga had everything except that, the Amiga did not have a graphical user interface capability. So at that point in my career I quit being the director of software engineering for the Amiga Computers Company and instead I went back to work being an engineer and I spent about seven months developing the user interface for the Amiga that I called Intuition.

Ron Nicholson

We'd have these big wall sized pieces of plastic that were essentially the layout for the chip and we were trying to put several tens of thousands of transistors down by hand and get it correct. An engineer nowadays would say without design tools that is impossible; you will never succeed; it will never work. So if you believe them the Amiga chipset is an impossibility that we managed to successfully create.

Now we also had to do this in a reasonable amount of time, several thousand transistors; a start-up company has a certain amount of funds.

It all came down to the trade shows and in particular the CES The Consumer Electronics Show where it was make or break time for Amiga. We had all these other interesting little novelties going but the truth was that we either delivered or we were going to run out of money. The money that we had going was good seed money that would get us to the point that we had something working but we had to go further, we had to find additional investors and turn it into a real system. The way to get additional investors was to show people that what we had thought we could get working was actually working.

And the place to do that was at CES, at the trade show. So it became one of those deadlines for us.

The CES was all-important; that it became make or break for us. That we knew that the investors, that the companies that would be interested in this. And would show enough interest and it would inspire the investors to give us the money that we needed; that we had to have a good showing at CES.

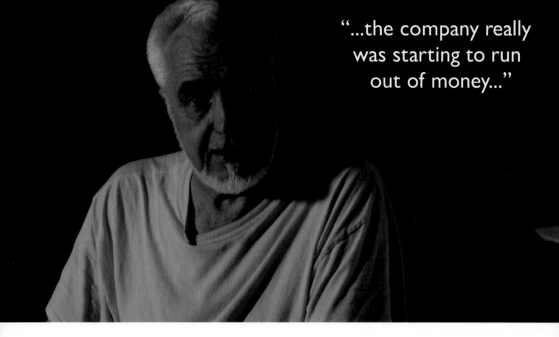

Rj Mical

At the same time the company really was starting to run out of money, seriously starting to run out of money. I had already started to become part of the executive half of the company at that point, so I was privy to a lot of the conversations they were having about how desperate things really were and how tight money was becoming.

In general this wasn't being discussed with the employees because we didn't want people to feel panicky and nervous and not work as well as they might or start looking for other jobs or something like that if they thought the company was going to fail.

So they kept it low-key, they didn't talk a lot about how important these trade shows were but we all sort of knew. I wasn't all that comfortable with keeping stuff from the employees and so I kind of told a lot of people some of what we're up against and why we needed to deliver.

"Dave Morris had a trade show he went to target and so we rushed ahead with the design."

Ron Nicholson

RJ Mical

As we were coming up to one of the early trade shows and we were both realising how desperate everything was and that we really needed to get our best foot forward. But also that we were so close and with just a little extra work there were so many cool things we could show then we ended up just working all night long.

We often worked all night long and Dale and I got into this thing where we would start playing rock music really loud in the middle of the night to help keep ourselves awake. And when you had to do something like cue up a five-minute compile instead of sitting there and potentially falling asleep you would stand up and dance.

And the two of us would take turns standing up and dancing three, four, five o'clock in the morning in the software lab to keep ourselves awake while we get on with our work. The Led Zeppelin was blaring loud and we're dancing.

Finally the day came that that we lost track of time and our co-workers start showing up to the office and and there's this loud music blaring out of the software lab. And they go back there to look to see what's going on and there's Dale and me dancing and dancing. We got the reputation then for being the dancing fools, that's where we got that nickname Dale and I were known as the dancing fools at Amiga because of that.

"What we did at Amiga was unprecedented then, the strange hardware rig that we put together to create the effect of the Amiga computer."

RJ Mical

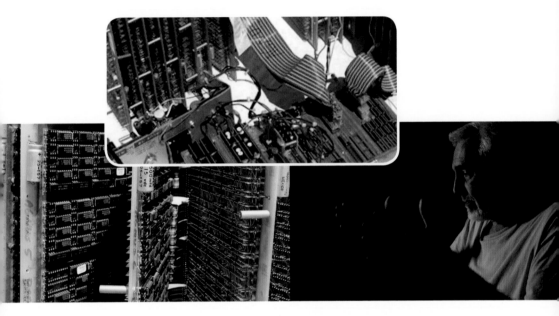

Ron Nicholson

We got lots of little parts that were individual NAND gates and registers, wire wrapped them together and try to get them running in order to find out if the logic circuits that we had drawn in paper actually work.

RJ Mical

Something as simple as an electrostatic shock would wipe them out. So they had them set up on this workbench in the software lab. They put chairs that forced you before you could approach the chips to walk along a certain corridor where you would step on this electrostatic pad that we had on the ground, that would take electro static electricity away from you so that you wouldn't zap the chips. Anyone that got anywhere near the chips had to step over this pad to get to the chip.

So we had this little corridor like an aisle down the centre of a church going to the chips at the end. And even better than that these chips the output of the chips we needed to make available to everyone that was in the software lab where we were. So we had these massive cables that were the graphics and audio output of these chips. We ran them up into the air and then they draped across where the the electrostatic pad was and went off to the rest of the software lab.

But where they draped across the walkway they draped down because it was loose and it made you kind of stoop a little bit. And as you would approach these Amiga stacks that one day would be the Amiga computer you were obliged to walk down this one corridor and just as you got up to the stacks you had to bow. You had to bow your head in order to get under the wires and it was like this religious experience that you would go through to approach the hardware.

And little did we know at the time that it was in fact quite a religious experience that we were creating not only for ourselves but for millions of people out there in the real world.

Ron Nicholson

My part in that was I actually hand wired the original two motherboards for the Amiga I did get one working and that was the one they used primarily to test the first set of breadboard emulators for the chipset. That was the one that we took down to one of the major trade shows the Consumer Electronics Show in Las Vegas.

RJ Mical

Everyone in the company worked their hearts out to get us to these trade shows and to have not just the technology but the best marketing presentation we could make.
And all the geniuses were there, the booth we put together for CES was just remarkable it was an amazing thing that had enough goodness on the outside to inspire everyone.
But if you were lucky enough to get an invitation into the inner sanctum of where the actual Amiga demo was going on then you were in for a real treat because that Amiga demo was so cool.

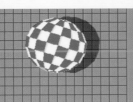

Ron Nicholson

A lot of people who saw the demo thought that we must have a fairly large mini computer or IBM mainframe in the next room emulating the output they saw because they said you can't do this and anything that would fit inside a personal computer.

RJ Mical

Our sales and marketing team at Amiga were just overjoyed with the success that we had. They decided they're going to take us out and give us this amazing dinner to celebrate the fact that we have had such an awesome first day at the Consumer Electronics Show. And we did we eat a lot of spaghetti and drink a lot of Chianti I suppose.

Then after that Dale and I were talking on our way back from the dinner and we realised there was still so much more we could do. And that if the first day was a success the second day could be even better if only we worked a little bit harder.

So the two of us instead of going back to our hotel rooms we went back to the CES trade show and we talked the guards into letting us get back into the booth. The two of us sat down in that booth and we stayed up all night long drinking warm beer and working on the demos to make the demos better so that on day two not only were they great but there are even a little bit greater than great. I mean added just a little bit more extra pizzazz and wonderment to them.

"Money was not available anymore."

Ron Nicholson

Towards the end of the chips being fabricated I think we actually got the chips back and they all worked. Money was not available any more. Stories that later came out that both Dave Morris and Jay miner took out mortgages on their house. I had only heard that later.

ANDY FINKEL
COMMODORE & AMIGA

Andy Finkel

I was actually still working on 64 and plus/4 things, working with various companies like Infocomm to help them port their stuff to the C64 and the plus/4 They all seemed to have a secret project going with some unnamed computer company. The locked room type stuff and while I was there hanging out with them there were things that they would not talk about.

Leonard Tramiel

Atari was in the process of losing two million dollars a working day. I don't know how they contacted dad somewhere on his trip; I think he was in Singapore or something like that. They said "please come to New York we want to talk to you about buying Atari".

And Sam said "we just bought Atari come home, come home now".

That was an interesting transition; graduate student in physics; honeymooner; vice president of software for a fortune 500 company.

RJ Mical

I hate to say it but I've never pulled this punch before. The way that Atari did business back then was miserable. I never abided by that way of thinking about business. That way of cutthroat making money and throwing people to the side, nothing matters more than being successful at making money I hated that.

They originally gave Amiga Computer money as a cheque. It was not a great deal but it was an okay deal and we were facing doom. Everyone was finally resigning themselves to the fate that Atari was going to get our baby from us. Then we would all be out of jobs and that this thing that we have dreamed of for all of those years was failing.

At the last moment when it seemed that there was no hope left, suddenly out of the blue came Commodore to the rescue. Commodore found out what Atari was offering us for the company and Commodore said,

"Oh we can do much better than that."

Rj Mical

They proposed a very nice rich dollar amount for the company that sounded great to all of us.

It was this awesome moment of negotiation where they offered us I think it was four dollars or four and a quarter or something I don't remember the exact number now.

Then Dave Morris our fearless leader turned to all of us and said "you know okay well here's the offer do you accept it's better than zero, it's better than Atari" and everyone that reported to him said "yes sounds good accept this deal'.

Then he turned back to Commodore and said, "no not quite enough we're going to have to pass on your offer".

And it's like 'Oh my goodness'. To have the courage to have a gun pointed to your head like that and still say no to the best offer you'd heard so far.

They offered him I think it was originally four and they offered him four and a quarter or something like that he said "okay" and the rest was history. Commodore bought the company and Atari's attempt to get their hands on the technology was foiled and Dave Morris returned the cheque to Atari.

I've heard recently that Atari still has that cheque ha-ha-ha! I would like the cheque but even just a photocopy would be lovely.

Andy Finkel

I discovered that Amiga and Commodore had just bought them.

Leonard Tramiel

Folk at Atari; and this is presumption, they certainly didn't tell me; thought alright we'll fund these guys and they'll make a nice machine except they're not be going to able to pay us back. So if they don't pay us within six months we own the technology.

RJ Mical

Commodore infused our company with cash and suddenly overnight we were productive citizens. We had powerful, big computers that we could use and we had mag tape drives built into the computer so we could back up our work on a nightly basis. All of this miracle stuff happened that made us more productive.

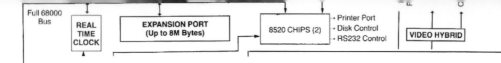

Andy Finkel

Right after the purchase happened within less than a month my group was actually sent out to California to work with the Amiga guys to get it ready for launch. We were doing things like printer drivers, device drivers, application software, just generally filling in where they were light on people.

RJ Mical

They themselves embrace the Amiga as the next generation that Commodore needed to go in. So it's this match made in heaven where 'oh it was great, the business was great, the hardware was great, our development environments became great.'

Gail Wellington

You had the development team in Los Gatos who had created a product that they thought would be a game machine. They could not produce it for the price that it would take to compete in the games market. Commodore acquired the company because they needed to move quickly into the next generation of computers and you had all these sales and marketing people on the East Coast with totally different ideas. It was quite a bit of friction.

GAIL WELLINGTON
COMMODORE & AMIGA

Jeff Porter

Amiga in California had this amazing technology that just needed to have a little bit of the low cost computer from Commodore and the high tech technology from Amiga and put that together to really come up with an amazing combination.

Andy Finkel

Everybody in Los Gatos got to go to the launch as a reward. We had this last-minute substitution of Graphicraft. Graphicraft Hat was a very early edition, it had some bugs and one of the bugs that still wasn't being tracked down was the flood fill. You could start a flood fill and it would flood; you can fill the screen and then keep going and fill the whole of the memory and so it crashed the computer.

So during the demo, during the training when Pariseau trained Andy Warhol he said 'don't do the flood fill'. And naturally during the demo, the live demo he does the flood fill.

The rows of engineers, we were all sitting together and we were like 'oh no' because we knew this couldn't work but somehow it did. It did not crash the machine and that's just one of those miracles that happen.

OPEN PAINTING

raphicraft V1.0

PLEASE SELECT A PAINTING NAME

boxes
kid-amiga
orangenix
shadowed

OR TYPE IN A NAME

kid-amiga

OK?   CANCEL

Amiga
AMIGA
A1000

Memory	1 MB
CPU Speed	7.14 Mhz
Sound	
Graphics	

Jeff Porter

My first job was to make the PAL
version of the Amiga 1000 and so I was the token guy from
Commodore in Westchester, Pennsylvania. They had to go
and talk to all the guys in Los Gatos and say alright we've got
to make a PAL video output from this computer because
the first Amiga was only NTSC.

Amiga 1000

Andy Finkel

Revolutionary at the time was its
multitasking of the whole. A lot of the
internal concepts, libraries, devices and so
on were just much more advanced than
most home computers had at that time.

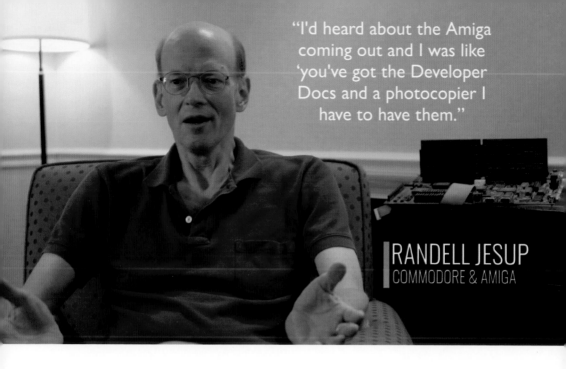

RANDELL JESUP
COMMODORE & AMIGA

Dave Haynie

The 128 was launched that summer and then the Amiga in the fall but I wanted to find out about it. There were these green books you could sign out, you had to put your name on them. And they had serial numbers and everything because they didn't want this information getting out. Bil Herd got one and I think the night or maybe the night after Bil Herd got his I stayed late and photocopied the whole thing so I could learn it.

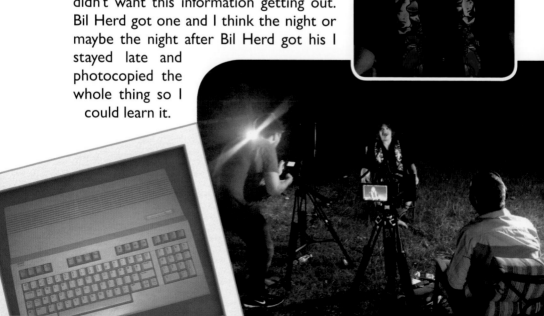

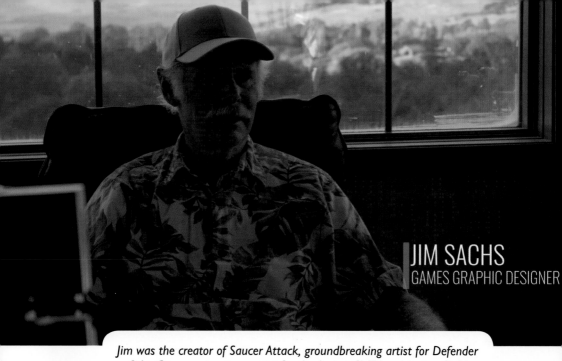

JIM SACHS
GAMES GRAPHIC DESIGNER

Jim was the creator of Saucer Attack, groundbreaking artist for Defender of the Crown, animations artist for the Amiga CDTV and Amiga CD32.

"So I did everything you see, every single surface.
Elevator goes down all three floors, if I ever build the thing.

'Deal with the plans' They said 'it's too complicated' so I said 'okay I'll build a model and you can go by that' so I did I built a model of whole thing and they took the measurements making the quarter inch equals a foot.
Everything in the model is actually to scale and then I had it there in the house and a bear got in before I had this door and destroyed it."

Crew

So this was a bear that did that?

Jim Sachs

He didn't like the design, I don't know.

Yes I did 'Defender of the Crown' on this, sitting in there.

We put speaker boxes there either side of the screen.

So I flew to Commodore headquarters in Westchester, Pennsylvania and grabbed one of the executives and I had a copy of my Saucer Tag game which looked pretty professional, I had nice packaging and stuff. On the basis of that they gave me a developer status on the Amiga.

I still had to buy one, they didn't give me an Amiga but they gave me all of the tools that RJ, Dale Luck and everybody had written in order to allow people to program on the Amiga. Went home and immediately started doing graphics that neither I or anybody else had ever seen before.

Michael Nurney

I saw 'Defender of the Crown' it was as I remember it a full-colour spread of the castle scene with a catapult of Defender of the Crown and it blew my socks off. It was a complete game changer to see something so beautiful, so artistic and almost photographic from a computer was something that I had never seen before. My mind was made up that I obviously needed an Amiga.

Now I couldn't afford an Amiga 1000 but fortunately Commodore did a wonderful thing they introduced the Amiga 500; which allowed my mum to buy me one in 1987 I think it was. What a wonderful machine the Amiga 500 was it brought the power of the Amiga to the masses. It really did create a software market; a hardware market and brought wonderful technology to the average person.

Jeff Porter

That launch of the Amiga 1000 in Europe was pretty amazing and that really started it all. And because of those relationships I had both with the factories and the vendors in the Far East, the engineers in Westchester, Pennsylvania, the engineers in Los Gatos, California and all the customers for the Amiga in Europe. That's what brought me to the alignment of the planets that got the Amiga 500 to say 'okay let me see if I can get this to a point where we can dramatically make a difference in terms of the cost of this product and make it available to a lot more people'.

"Defender of the Crown was the scenario, it was written by Kellyn Beck and he approached Bob Jacob who was a producer at the time with the idea of doing one of the first Amiga games as a cinematic game based on the movie Ivanhoe."

Jim Sachs

Amiga	AMIGA
A500	

Memory	512 KB
CPU Speed	7.09 Mhz
Sound	
Graphics	

1987

David Pleasance

Batman of course set the whole barometer because it was a movie that was anticipated probably like never before and probably never since as that one particularly was. I've got the most amazing respect for ocean software having the guts to go along with that idea but that's where the whole idea, where the concept is correct something which is bigger than the sum of the parts. And we specifically had the Amiga as a very small 'oh by the way there's an Amiga in the Box'.

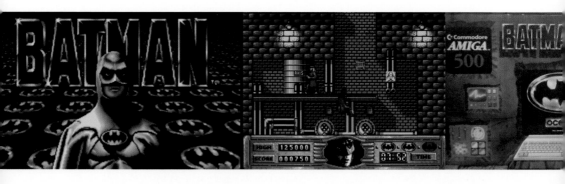

It wasn't about selling; if you remember I came up with a concept 'from now on we don't sell computers we sell dreams' and that's what we did and everything we produced was a dream.

Andy Finkel

We had Dale luck come to Westchester, we had Bart Whitebook come to Westchester so we didn't want to lose the software guys but unfortunately couldn't help it, some people moved on.

Dave Haynie

"There's a lot more to do on the Amiga 2000 because nothing had been done really the 500 I think at that point was pretty close to finished."

Trevor Dickinson

A lightning storm in Texas; the Lightning came through the phone line and zapped my 128D Fortunately I had insurance so with the insurance money I purchased my first Amiga, it was an Amiga 2000.
So you could see my progression to Amiga was actually an act of God or at least that's what it said in the insurance policy.

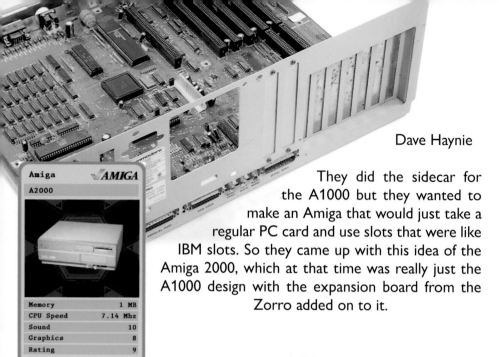

Amiga	AMIGA
A2000	

Memory	1 MB
CPU Speed	7.14 Mhz
Sound	10
Graphics	8
Rating	9

Dave Haynie

They did the sidecar for the A1000 but they wanted to make an Amiga that would just take a regular PC card and use slots that were like IBM slots. So they came up with this idea of the Amiga 2000, which at that time was really just the A1000 design with the expansion board from the Zorro added on to it.

Jeff Porter

At the same time that I was working on the Amiga 500 there was a team in Braunschweig, Germany building an Amiga 2000 because the 1000 was trying to service two markets with one computer. It couldn't really do that too well. It's too expensive for the home and not expandable enough for the serious user. So you ended up with a 500 and 2000 and that was really a pivotal step in the Amiga to make that successful.

You had people like NewTek that made the Video Toaster in the United States. They could do amazing things with a 2000 because now they can plug a card in. And you had high school and college kids that could afford to buy an Amiga and get into programming or graphic design where they couldn't do that before.

Randell Jesup

I ended up getting a job at Commodore working for Andy Finkel initially. I had thought about cutting my hair before that because I had long hair at the time. It's like 'I think I'm just going to go down and see if they accept me as I am' and they did and so I and Bryce Nesbitt both started around the same time.

Jeff Porter

When the 600 was introduced; by the way it was supposed to be called the A300 because it was supposed to cost less.
It turns out that the team of engineers that they put on designing this cost reducing 600 couldn't out cost reduce Jeff's 500 so they ended up having to call that a 600 because it actually cost more.
They still went into production with it but now you've got two computers that are pretty similar and how do you market that?
So the Germans saw this and they said "well why do we need a 600 when the 500 is cheaper and does at least as good a job?

Randell Jesup

Mehdi made the decision that probably put the final nail in the coffin of Commodore. This was to launch the 1200 with double A but not commit to enough chips to make the entire production for Christmas. Instead he built 300,000 old chips for the 500s, most of which stayed in the warehouse because who wants to buy the old machine when you can get the brand-new machine with more colours and faster processor and everything else.

Amiga
A1200

Memory	2 MB
CPU Speed	14 Mhz
Sound	
Graphics	

Jeff Porter

The 1200 wasn't actually available in volume until December and so you pretty much missed the Christmas season. So if you introduced the 1200 in November and you only had a limited supply you're only going to frustrate people at Christmas time that they can't buy the computer that they really want to buy.

"A lot of things were going wrong all at the same time in those days and it was pretty obvious to us all. It's just your technology people and you've sort of got along thinking that every problem is solved by technology and it's certainly not."

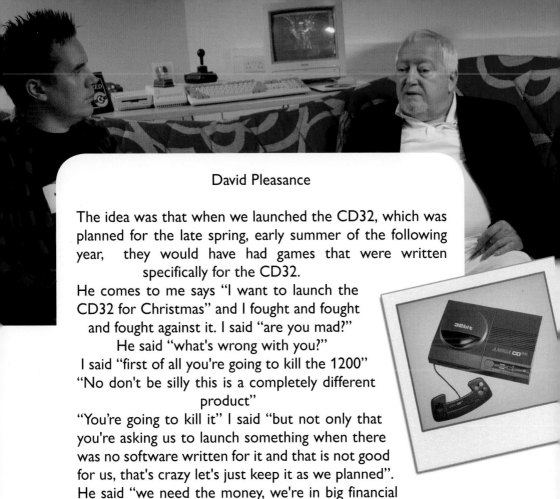

David Pleasance

The idea was that when we launched the CD32, which was planned for the late spring, early summer of the following year, they would have had games that were written specifically for the CD32.

He comes to me says "I want to launch the CD32 for Christmas" and I fought and fought and fought against it. I said "are you mad?"

He said "what's wrong with you?"

I said "first of all you're going to kill the 1200"

"No don't be silly this is a completely different product"

"You're going to kill it" I said "but not only that you're asking us to launch something when there was no software written for it and that is not good for us, that's crazy let's just keep it as we planned".

He said "we need the money, we're in big financial trouble, we need the extra sales".

And I kept saying to him "they're not going to be extra sales; they may replace 1200 sales but they're not going to be extra sales" he wouldn't listen.

Dave Haynie

So Commodore had this nasty habit of announcing bad news after the close of business on Friday. So they announced their bankruptcy after the close of business on Friday while a good portion of us were at Mike Sinz' wedding and did not know that.

We got to Randell's house and they had a news article taped on the door so everyone who went in would notice that note that Commodore had gone out of business the night before.

David Pleasance

We got a copy of the announcement that was made to the worldwide press that's how significant we weren't. We just got a copy the same as everybody else did 'Commodore announces liquidation and so on. They hadn't even got the guts to pick up the phone and say 'thanks for all your help but you know it didn't work, we're declaring bankruptcy'.
But there again I'm not surprised about that I didn't have any regard for the management, apart from a fondness for Irving Gould but I had no regard for the management side of Commodore International. So I'm not surprised at how they handled things.

Gail Wellington

I left before the end. I was lucky I got out whilst there was still severance money; my stock options still had some value and not only that but I left and went, without paying admission, to the Software Publicists Association meeting. I went into a multimedia conference and I was sitting in the audience; having been multimedia personality the year in the UK a few years before; and there's this panel discussion and the moderator at the end of the panel says "Gail, we have the mother of multimedia application sitting in the audience, Gail is there anything you would like to say?" and I thought 'oh my...'.
So I took a deep breath, did one of the hardest things I've ever done in my life, I stood up and said "yes I'd like to say I'm looking for a job" - and I got one.

"I didn't know that we would be as successful as we were and how many millions of lives we ended up touching with the thing that we had created."

RJ Mical

We were able to create a machine that was low cost, so very powerful. It took the industry by storm for the longest time and was the video editing platform of the world. That's what we wanted, we wanted to create a machine that anyone could use and that anyone could afford; that anyone could understand.

I didn't know that we would be as successful as we were and how many millions of lives we ended up touching with the thing that we had created.

And I often get emails from people who say something like 'hi just wanted to drop in and thank you for that Amiga computer thing that you did; it inspired me to get a job in computer graphics or it inspired me to get a job in commercial development or game development'

And I would get these wonderful letters from people that, each and every one of them, is like gold to me.

It validates what we believed from the beginning that we could create a machine that would open up people to new capabilities that they had. To reveal to themselves the sorts of things they might be able to do with their lives. We were so successful at that I'm delighted to say, I'm proud to say that part of our mission we were able to accomplish.

"I'm at Amiga 32 Germany and just bloody look at it. How many people are here? It's just absolutely crazy."

RAVI ABBOTT
THE RETRO HOUR

Ron Nicholson

They are still showing brand-new software they are writing for a computer that I developed 34 years ago that I thought would merely be a museum piece.
The gaming industry and the Amiga fans have kept it alive in a way that I could have never imagined.

Kenny McAlpine

I think that that 8-bit sound is the musical equivalent of candy. It speaks of childhood but it speaks of something more. It speaks of a kind of uplifting, joyous celebration of everything that childhood represents. It is safety, it is warmth and above all it's fun.

Chris Huelsbeck

There has been quite a nice retro revival over the last few years. There's constantly games being released like Steam and other platforms and that recreates the vibe of the old days.

Rob Hubbard

I sometimes look back and think if I'd have known this stuff was going to last this long I'd probably have taken it a bit more seriously.

"This crazy room with 500 plus people here in Germany.
Thirty years later celebrating that amazing computer and the technology that went into it."

Jeff Porter

Mark Knight

You'll have this purple, throbbing Amiga monster in all your houses controlling everything. Let's get rid of these Macintosh's and these PC's and IPad's and all that. Let's go back to the roots of Amiga.

Bill Winters

We started a YouTube channel called the 'Guru Meditation' named after the famous guru meditation error you get when your Amiga crashes and we have a sense of humour.

Mark Cale

I'm from system 3
What does Commodore mean to me? Well it means passion and it was a life changer for us all our best games came from the Commodore 64 and the Amiga

Chris Zimmerman

They can look back and say 'oh I had one of those' or 'I wanted something like that' so it's really fun for me to be able to share what I have with everybody here.

ANDY & DEAN
RETRO COMPUTER MUSEUM

Andy Spencer & Dean Payne

My name's Andy Spencer and I'm Dean Payne and we are the Retro Computer Museum.

"Next year March 2018 the Home Computer Museum will be open in Helmond, The Netherlands."

BART VAN DEN AKKER
HOME COMPUTER MUSEUM

HOME
COMPUTER
MUSEUM

www.HomeComputerMuseum.nl

Marvin Droogsma

Me and some friends even visiting the Amiga 30 in Mountain View, California; because why not? And then to England, Germany and everywhere it was crazy.

ATE VAN DER MEER
COMMODORE/AMIGA SALES

"I'm that passionat
about Commodor
and Amiga that I
engraved my iPhon
with the Amiga log

"I'm going to make sure that my grandson knows about Amiga"

Trever Dickinson

Trevor Dickinson

We're currently in Cardiff in Wales attending the A-EON DEVCON 2017. I'm hopeful of the work we're doing and the work the community is doing as a whole will ensure the future of the Amiga for the next 10, 20, 30 years and I'm going to make sure that my grandson knows about Amiga and actually will have his own.

"I'm here at revival 2017 the Rivals with Dave Perry from Gamesmaster on stage behind me."

Dan Wood

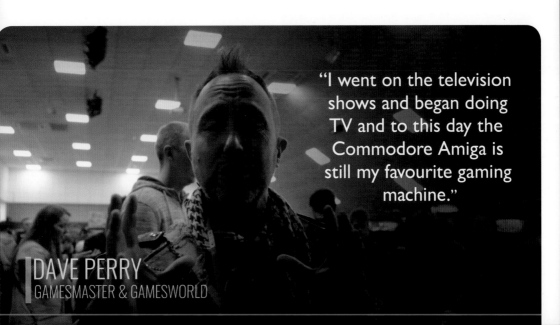

"I went on the television shows and began doing TV and to this day the Commodore Amiga is still my favourite gaming machine."

DAVE PERRY
GAMESMASTER & GAMESWORLD

Paul Cole

My time with the Commodore 64 was usually at my friend's house. I used to go over there every day, every weekend to play some games!

Mat Allen

There was this lovely shiny, beige bread bin sitting on the table with a few games. How little they knew what was going to happen for the next thirty years hence.

Kim and Angelo

This is the 1541 Ultimate II. What you can do with this is you can connect an SD card or a USB flash drive to load Commodore 64 games.

Gideon Zweijtzer

I think right now we're looking at about four thousand Ultimate II that are now in the field so that's quite a lot.

"They wanted to spend their fifty-pences and two pounds and three pounds whatever. I can't remember how much these games were. They wanted to make this device do something that doesn't exist today."

Anthony Clarke

Warren Pilkington

I got my first Commodore 64 and it was the first release of the 64C.
So I had the slim line model and to begin with. That slimline model I still have and it still works to this day.

Michal Taszycki

64 Bites is a series of short videos released weekly that introduces various aspects of programming Commodore 64.

Detlef Hastik

This is where mega comes in. This is the original C65 as mentioned; the one which the Zed Yago demo was coded on. And this is what we have made, it's basically the same.

"Hi everybody Zach Weddington here; director of Viva Amiga and I am on the set of the Commodore Story."

ZACH WEDDINGTON
DIRECTOR - VIVA AMIGA

David Murray

I keep the actual C64 here for occasional testing even though I do most of my development on the modern computer. And I keep this old TV here because it actually has a really blurry picture and so it's actually helped me redefine some of the graphics a little bit to make them a little easier to view.

DAVID MURR
THE 8 BIT GUY

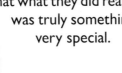

"Billion to nothing and just about three that's a strange kind of genius that Mehdi Ali'.
Because that was a billion dollar company; three years down the tubes to nothing."

Dave Haynie

David Pleasance

We are looking back on the retro scene from technology of 30 years ago but even today the technology of tomorrow is being developed. And they're using the Amiga technology.

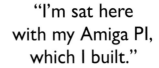

"I'm sat here with my Amiga PI, which I built."

James Zeun

Mark Barrett

It just shows you that what they did really was truly something very special.

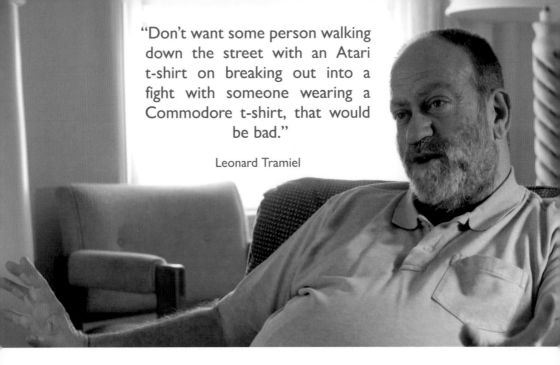

"Don't want some person walking down the street with an Atari t-shirt on breaking out into a fight with someone wearing a Commodore t-shirt, that would be bad."

Leonard Tramiel

Andy Finkel

'Jack Buster's who ya gonna call' is an original Amiga t-shirt; very rare. This is actually from workbench 2.0. Computer people at that time had a bad sense of humour.
This is the famous 'Commodore supports its floppy's'.

Leonard Tramiel

So that trip that I mentioned, the 60th anniversary of the clearing of the Lodz Ghetto, there were my parents, my aunt and uncle, my mother's sister's husband and a bunch of that generations kids and then that generations kids.
And there's a wonderful picture of us taken in Birkenau at the end of the railway line.

MARTIN CHESSE
THE NATIONAL MUSEUM OF COMPUTING

Bletchley Park - UK

Martin Chesse

I am here at the National Museum of Computing, which is located in the historic Block H of Bletchley Park.
So behind me is the Harwell Dekatron - its original name.
It is now the world's oldest working computer.

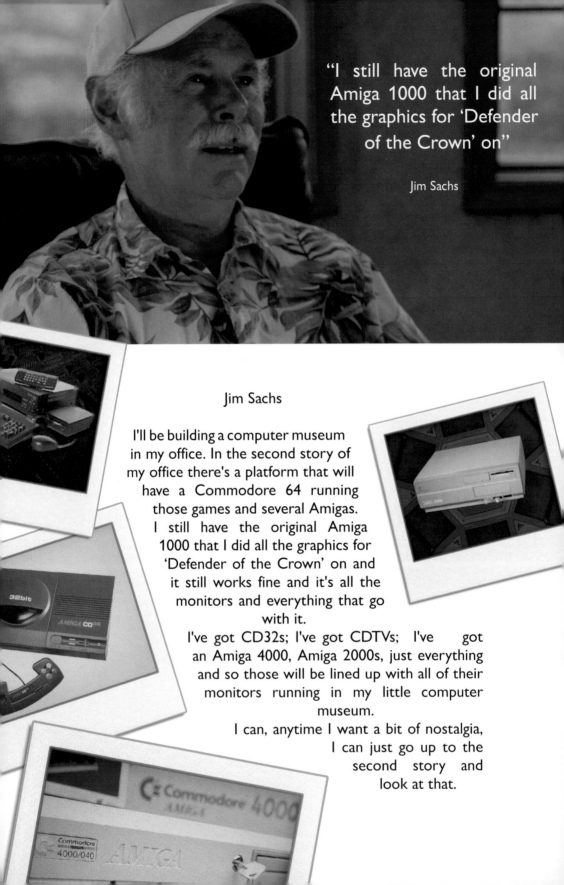

"I still have the original Amiga 1000 that I did all the graphics for 'Defender of the Crown' on"

Jim Sachs

Jim Sachs

I'll be building a computer museum in my office. In the second story of my office there's a platform that will have a Commodore 64 running those games and several Amigas. I still have the original Amiga 1000 that I did all the graphics for 'Defender of the Crown' on and it still works fine and it's all the monitors and everything that go with it.

I've got CD32s; I've got CDTVs; I've got an Amiga 4000, Amiga 2000s, just everything and so those will be lined up with all of their monitors running in my little computer museum.

I can, anytime I want a bit of nostalgia, I can just go up to the second story and look at that.

"Commodore indeed was a pioneering company and changed many, many lives including mine. The retro scene over the last few years seems to be growing and growing and all I want to say is you should embrace your inner 8-bit and 16-bit passion and continue on the retro ride."

Steven Fletcher

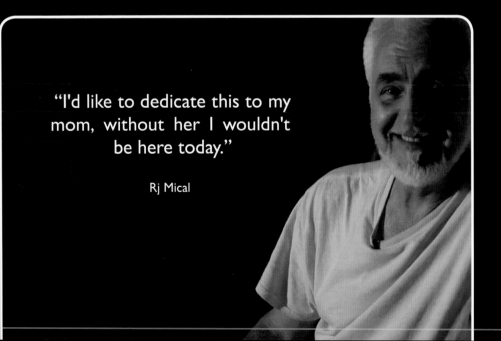

"I'd like to dedicate this to my mom, without her I wouldn't be here today."

Rj Mical

MISSION COMPLETE

CANNON FODDER

ELITE: A FANTASTIC VOYAGE OF DISCOVERY AND ADVENTURE
ELITE
RAINBIRD

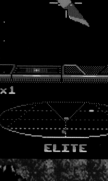
x1
ELITE

AMES POND 2 RoboCod
HE'S MEAN, HE'S GREEN, HE'S PART MACHINE
MILLENNIUM

WARNING
WE ARE NOT RESPONSIBLE FOR:
LOSS OF SANITY
LOSS OF HAIR
LOSS OF SLEEP
PSYGNOSIS

OUT 9 IN

THE SECRET OF MONKEY ISLAND
A GRAPHIC ADVENTURE BY RON GILBERT
Pick up   Use
Look at   Push
Talk to   Pull
Walk to

RAINBOW ISLAND
ocean

100000

ONVED 0-0 DEBRECE

Sensible SOCCER
1992/3 SEASON EDITION SENSIBLE SOCCER
European Champions
MUSIC BY CAPTAIN SENSIBLE!

WIZKID

WIZKI

KICKSTARTER BACKERS

Linda Fletcher
Bernard Fletcher
Klaus Moster
Daniel Auger
Mike Redman
Steven Gailey
Marc Alexander Grundke
Graham Dawes
Raymond Day
Edmund Vosik
Kevin Stilwell
Marcel Beringer
John Lomax
Tobias Graw
Jeppe Schmidt
Dave Mitchell
Brian Goubeaux
Marc Oberhuser
Jeremiah Nellis
Magnus Andersson
Michael J Nurney
Anthony Caulfield
Gavin Rye
Mitch Miner
Paul Moore
Rory Frederick Joscelyne
Marco Gubitzer
Rick Umali
Joakim Schã
Ed Piotrowski
Travis Estell
Jasper Brekelmans
Darwyn Brown
Nikolas Engstrã
Per-Anders Josefsson
Francois
Jonathan Lavigueur
Fredrik Zetterlund
Julian Lewis-Booth
Kenneth W Reid
Gemma Bright
John Rodriguez Ii

Bryan Beaulieu
Michael J Tedone
Marc Almond
David Youd
Draugluin
Carlos Catano
Brian Pittman Logiudice
Brielle Harrison
Michal Lokåia
James Burrows
Gene Schoensee
Stefan Blixth
Quyen Wickham
Fredrik Waage
Ed Green
David Martin
Matt Forrest
Florian Berger
Retrograde77
Tony Muller
Harri Kauhanen
Rudolf Petry
Daniel Tippmann
Nick C.
Wojciech Jakã Bczyk
Gabriel Bergqvist
Johannes Musikant
Zhool
Cerritus-Psittacus
Pasi Hã Nninen
Rkenter
David
Maximilian Meyer
Tieg Zaharia
Emanuele Iannone
Ian Matthews
Matt Dale
Jacob Roeland
Neil Mansell
Raffaele Sclafani
Maik Massmann
Brooke Phillips

Vassilis Pateras
Traal
Piotr Esden-Tempski
Haukevb
Juhani Kantola
Frank O
Giorgio Pomettini
Cezz
Lee Hickin
Robert Blank
Marcus Linkert
Stefan Gagne
Magnus
Ron Solo
Jason Legault
Aaron Hackney
Causal Bit Games
David Munoz
Brandon Williams
William Langford
Mark Elliott
Sebastian Mach
Tim Byrne
Superdos
Darkdust
Lane Daughtry
Jason Rose
Michael Szul
Will Williams
Ryan Hidalgo
Matt Smith
Steven-Eric Poulin
Stirring Dragon Games
Allan Callaghan
Stephen Day
Jonathon Lowe
Serge Wallagh
Maheka
Anders Persson
Andy Gilbert
Daniel Tootill
Luke Dickinson

Michael Drach
Jud Richardson
Splinecl
Donny White
Julian Laufer
Sebastian Kobiela
Mark Mcdonald
Dane
Fredrik Blomqvist
John Jones
James Kelleher
Travers Cleeman
John Berger
Stephen Bennett
Carey Yingling
Neil Davis
Nathan "Jintolyn" Jones
Järn Tillnes
Anthony Clarke
C64Audio.Com
Geir Eivind Mork
Tim Neumann
Brick Dad
The Sonsie Bogle
Dan Shaurette
Gereon Faäÿbender
Rick Huizinga
Byron
Olle Johansson
Mikael Abrahamsson
Alexain
Alain Deschenes
Mdrake42
Delphin64
Richard Karsmakers
Jari Pakarinen
Neil Blakely
Superrune
Dukestah
Nate
Simo Koivukoski
Tommi Saarela
Jeff
Johannes Rath
Sebastien Brassard
Timothy Blanks

Michel Van Geel
Tayger
John Fritz
Justadude
Peter Greene
Turo Heikkinen
Mike Fleischner
David Baker
Ronny Arild
Pauli "Pave"
Haarnimo "Mentman"
Steve Ruston
Gary Kind
Falko Loeffler
Alan J Stuart
Daniel Provencio
Steven Stanton
Rabih Ghandour
Rob Hayles
Michael K.
Martin Knizia
Raphael Meyer
Nicola Piovesan
Geir Skjeret
Ablackfyre
Daniel
Sebastian Cheshire
Todd
Daniel Spreadbury
Brian K. Perry
Claus Morell
Peter Neubauer
Stephen Paltrineri
Chand Svare Ghei - Moonknight
Arjan De Vries
Daniel Willis
Derek Vickers
Irowboat
Simon Henstock
Peter Giokaris
David Given
Francis Erdman
Diego Barros
Emil "Angryant" Johansen
Raphael Falkoff
Derek J. Balling

Christopher
Paul Allen Pentecost
Tom Degroh
Michael Von Tessin
Mike Lonesky
David Lengeler
Axel Buerkle
Battika
Eric Sloof
Mirva Luukkainen
Douglas Robbins
Hdima
Ceri Stagg
Antonio Bernardini
Giovanni Cardona
Wei-Ju Wu
Richard Michael Smith
James Murphy
Dietmar Schinnerl
Hallvard A. Ulsund
Mercy Ground Creations
Deadsanity
Presley Martin
Stephanie
Scott Finney
Stephen Greszczyszyn
Andrew Geppert
Mike Mgarcia
Matthew Garside
Stewart Dunn
Jaakko Keränen
Chordian
Sandburg
Jon Henry
Geert Poels
Jagdflanker
Christian Gendreau
Robbie Gieze
Kox
Joseph Hill
Josha Munnik
Patrick Beck
Devon Hubner
Oliver Lind
Stelios K
Barry Christian

Hermit Hacker
Niek Veenstra
Per Nielsen
Neil Pritchard
Serge-Eric Tremblay
Paul Chapman
Gordonwalker
Philip Bruce
Andrew Eick
Jamie Ketskemety
Gert Hansen
Amplitude Problem
Stefan Amann
Fowling
Alistair
John Boysen Trãholt
Matteo Matassoni
Andre Moeri
Imre Olajos
Andreas Beck
Robert Garan
Sn00Ze
Tuomas Salminen
Adrian Mules
Therootofallevil
Rikard Ed
Alexander Von Schlinke
Harry Culpan
Erik Johannessen
Jeromeb
Richard
Paul
Ivan Richardson Ii
Aaron Mcfadzien
Paul Martin
Markus Teubner
Tom Ludwig
Pisco
Ish Ot Jr
John Bourne
Krupky
Carey Bishop
The Arrow
Scott Johnson
Christian W Frank
John Kenneth Grytten

Karsten Dambekalns
Joseph H
Stuart Hunt
Rusty Keele
Rene Thomsen
Mike Desmarais
Asbjãrn Ulsberg
Nathan Campos
Kenneth Bill
Jason Short
Vince Mirabella
Ross Williams
Matt Borum
Keith Mashinter
Stephen Barriball
Geijer
Jonas Schmid
Ross Lipenta
Ycswyd
Colin Lawlor
Dave Test
Branko Novosel
Marcos Genaro
Shauna Sargent
Kamil Burzynski
Michael Beverland
Matt A Finnegan
Mirko Palmer
Ramond De Vrede
Stuart Shields
Brian Eddy
Javier Casares
Panagis Lefteratos
Wouter Snijders
Thomas Jeising
Jon Shute
Jacob Nielsen
Marcus Pirron
James Bell
David Major
Peter Modl
Juha Alaniemi
Edi Budimilic
Mr Scott Macdonald
Jason Chau
Martin Seeger

Mark White
Akyol Tarimci
Jamas Enright
Rob Dabell
Ashley Dawson
John Rorland
Paul Driver
Andrew Gordon
Jeffrey Farnsworth
Jens Kristian Jensen
Charles Houck
Stuart Brittain
Graham W Wãbcke
Rob Frood
John M Osborne
Tim Kane
Jonathan Chan
Joe Yaksich
Margaret St John
Oliver Wright
P Burne
Micke Holm
Kuba Tyszko
Mr Edward Dawes
Jade Pearce
Alex Edge
J. Matt Peterson
Jesse C Smillie
Daniel Stephens
Klaus Post
Boris Mateå¡ln
Michael Brandvold
David Macpherson
Howie Schwartz
Marcus Albers
Robert Crossfield
Michael P Cassera
Henning Leutz
Michal Skladnikiewicz
Jonathan Abrams
Ross Mackinnon
Mathias Harnerud
Answer
Mads Troest
Michael Keith
Kai Luedeking

Gregory Saunders
Richard Prokesch
David J Kochbeck
Kevin Burke
Eric Schätzlein
Torstein Rodset
Hakon Sporck
Peter Mattsson
Chris Foulds
Steven Saunders
Cetin Mericli
Jonathan Kaye
Andy Townsend
Hãctor Juan Lãpez
Jeroen Van Jaarsveld
Tyler K Sigman
Lars Klaeboe
Daniel J Sabroe
Jani Pullinen
Kurt Shultz
Jason Warnes
Benjamin Schmaus
Arne Neumann
Matt Huffman
Kevin Foss
Gary Stringer
Konrad Klinkner
Benjamin Thomson
Matthew Barrett
Manuel Friedrich
Thierry Tranchina
Lee Stoneman
Juergen Szolay
James Greaves
Santiago Venneri
Sebastien Clavet
Horst Thieme
Buranszki Gergely
Richard Smith
Mike Joblin
Anders Jensen
Michael Knoll
Asher Feldman
Koni Weber
Tamas Kalman
Andy Hessler

Lapierre Cyril
Sirivong Bounlith
Gergo Erdi
Hory Fabien
Olivier Vigneresse
Mike King
Hongrui Guo
John Durnall
Trey Aughenbaugh
Jeffrey Ciccone
Goetz Salzmann
Chris Saguisag
Keir Ford
Sm De Miranda
Marvin Murdock
Mike Shema
Justin Elliott
Kristian Svanes
Austin Robinson
Tomas Wikstrã
Klaus Timmermann
Ian Cunningham
Stefan Hammarstedt
Bieno Marti
Steve Green
Ignacio Planas Beamonte
Tomas Matys
Vanja Utne
Rocco Di Leo
Brian Juul Nielsen
Mike Whelan
Mark Hellewell
Johnny Tomic
Dean Froley
Bjãrn Johannesson
Edward Fitzpatrick
Peter Mcquillan
Jakob Bakke
Warren Lapworth
John Moody
Tom Christensen
Paul Moore
Richard Vallender
Russell Howard
Justin Paul
Michelle Mckinney

Lee Jordan
Ernst Krogtoft
Darren Webber
Andrew Stewart
Tim Lawson
Daniel Mackey
Mark Robin
Andrew Bugenis
Franck Sauer
Eero Konttaniemi
Twan Claassen
Oivind Ekeberg
Marcin Prochnicki
Peter Karlsson
Serge De Roo
Thierry Mazzoleni
Paul Ryan
Lefevre Christophe
Jaakko Nikunen
Paul Townsend
Anthony Cillo
F De Gans
Yann Barthelemy
Justin Cremin
Joerg Droege
Finn Renard
Sherri Densmore
David Bulwer
Thomas Lesvang
David Tafulo Jorge
Pistelli Maurizio
Dr Michael C Tanner
Bernhard Lukas
Gareth Darby
Andre Bergei
Paul Kitching
Henrie Vos
Fredrik Jorevall
Aaron Wald
Iain Rockliffe
Anthony Beckett
Kirk Herlitz
Arthur Chocholacek
Mike Robertson
Jonas Olsson
Hilaire Eric

Patrick Becher
Barrie Clark
Michael Kuppinger
Terje Häiback
Heather Kent
M Van Schendelen
Marko Däring
Richard Sheller
Moraux Benoit
Peter Badrick
Scott Julian
Tom Pedersen
Pekka Saarimaa
Johan Svensson
Skevos Mavros
Philip T. Reichert
Wojciech Saladajczyk
Antti Mustakangas
John Gasson
Melanie Fritsch
Matthew Tuffin
Michael Winn
Alexander Young
Stephen Stuttard
James Thomson
Bart Pellens
Tuan Nguyen
Gary Mcnab
Sven Harvey
Knut Kraushaar
Iain Roberts
Bruno Lopes
Stephane Raymond
Kymon Zonias
Bjärn Melbãe
Raymond Homme Ingebretsen
Joakim Bergman
Daniel Murphy
Arion Lawrence
Claudio Perfumo
Raymond Green
Tony Brice
Jakob Kjäller
Thomas Wirtzmann
Richard Davey
George Sokianos

Herr Markus Werner
Nicolas Clement
Kim Beck
Lee Pearson
Brian R. Boisvert
John Myron
Mark Paul Corcoran
Fuchs Joel
Marco Hendrikse
Thomas Karlsson
Tony Law
Steve Williams
Tony Peters
Frank Fay
Thomas Jeserofsky
Christian Wikander
Sebastian Kranz
Jochen Seidler
David Martin
Suzanne Scherrer
Jonathan Bentley
Claudio Marro Filosa
Jan-Erik Sundh
Martin Lee White
Sune Loeje
George Papadontas
Bjärn Jonsson
Andrew Mcallister
Christian Witt
Lehuãã Charly
Gaetano Campagna
Erik Elsom
Tony Cappellini
Billy Hanna
Francisco J. Estãvez
Rick Reynolds
George Haritonidis
Darren Shoesmith
Chris Wilkins
Louãt Yann
Vesko Gavrilov
Mark Ambrose
Marco Bonadonna
Daryl Bidewell
Ryan Chenery
Frank Eivind Rundholt

Jeffrey Wittenhagen
Alonso J Nunez Gonzalez
Marcin Kozinski
Rune Vendler
Marek Kastelovic
Miguel Laiz
William Prince
Glenn Ozburn
Briatte Fabien
Prieur Joel
Dieter Marchsreiter
Peter Hjulskov Kristensen
Werner Rott
Zeno Guarienti
Kuo-Jen Yuan
Csãpe Szabolcs
Andrew Coughlan
Jan Markus Mãuer
Robert Quenet
Johannes Schaefer
Joel Calippe
Mike Machian
Clint Pohler
Pierre Fontaine
Vincent G Barbara
Michael Swanson
Peter Tirsek
Kay Bensberg
David Petyt
Eric Smalling
Fabio Zanicotti
Richard Statham
Roger Schuncken
Michael Bãhme
Harri Tolvanen
Stephen Kew
Nicolas Sallin
Mark Spieckerman
Patrice Scheidt
Nicholas Ledgard
Vladimir Lusik
Gareth Robinson
Jarkko Lehtola
Daniel Von Schallen
Gregory Soravilla
Glenn Cline

James Barnard
Michael Tedder
Stuart Clenton
Steve Jones
Alexander Ryan
Anthony Jarvis
Markus Marion
Logan Brown
Lars Erik Johnsrãd
John Dijkman
Claus Gahrn
Alex Hopson
Brian Kleinke
Roy Stanfield
Neil Evans
Richard Lupton
Dan Larshagen
Thomas Bouvrette
Rogier Van Der Veen
Robin Moojen
Kev Mccullagh
Jeremy Mitchell
Ian Muttoo
Ian Nurser
Fiona Ewings
Jarkko Lehti
Oliver Giesemann
Mark Marchione
Sebastian Szade
John Paul Barrick
Rick Geraedts
Nikolaos Karypidis
Robin Elvin
Tandlã¦Gen.Dk
Stuart Williams
Nathanial Vella
Christian Sturm
Jãrn Rune Jakobsen
Nicholai Juul Hansen
Rameez Athaulla
Francesco Brolli
Kurt Geisel
Pelle Larsson
Steven Allen
Rick Mallen
Timo Klinga

Riccardo Martoglia
Darren Townsend
Michael Mayerhofer
Paul Hesford
Carsten Bãrmann
Kenneth Jãnsson
Paul Olszewski
Stuart Lofthouse
Wayne Bowman
Michael Hall
Adam Wade
Braden Manning
Steinar Midtskogen
Sheryl Knight
Richard Jinks
Juergen Probe
Brian Dueholm Olesen
Stefan Dorschner
Koen De Brabander
Joao Carlos Garcia Arias
Jackie Mason
Kai-Uwe Nielsen
Mr Corin Hamilton
Damian Manning
Ricky Fong
Matteo Pascolini
Giles Moorhouse
Thomas Beck
Petr Vanäk
Angelo Houben
Eric Hays
Robin Van Der Hoeven
John Zurawski
Keir Fraser
Gunnar Andersson
Florian Lobsien
Joni L-Haikarainen
Jeffrey B Leggett
Shayne Fotheringhame
Lee Olivares
Greg Burrell
Geir Teigo
James Dyer
Andreas Kassel
Daren Klamer
Brian Mora

Jason Robertson
Paul Kubiszyn
Shaun Stephenson
Mikkel Graugaard Hansen
Steven Evans
Aaron Schnuth
Wayne Ashworth
Michael Isbitski
Roger Isaac
Kevin Starr
Bill Winters
Paul Heller
Matt Smith
Markus Tillmann
Ronck Robert
Toni Caven
Kofi Tsamenyi
Erik Pede
Christian Lucas
Justin Cripe
Michael Warmbold
Milton Watkins
Dr Robert Lawlor
Mauricio Vives
Chris Baker (Retrochrisb)
Andrew Brown
Michael Dellapia
Daniel Yaã±Ez
Scott Burge
Martin Lehmann
Myles Cameron-Smith
Billy Smithers
Bart Van Den Akker
Fox Cutter
Luca Argentiero
Markus Liukka
Todd Lawson
Anthony Charles Ball
Travis Howell
Sylvain Rousseau
Jãrg Weese
Scott Bishop
Karl Todd
Lorenz David
Mat Allen
Carlo Luciano Bianco

Kyle Good
Edoardo Auteri
Charles Atencio
Stefan Riemer
Paul Newport
SJ Van Rooijen
Keith Day
Rolf Scheimann
Tim Daeleman
Henrik Teinelund
Amy Humphries
Thomas Finnerup
David Bilowus
Marcin Segit
Mike Henderson
Stevan Rankic
Frank Eisenwiener
Krystof Cioch
Robohaus
Stuart Polkamp
Paul Harrington
Brian Handscomb
Ramon Fasel
Ronny Wagener
Nick Lines
Robert Troughton
Carsten Degn
Mark Jowett
Jeffrey Edwards
Michael Mitchell
Marco Das
Jose Olivenca
Ken Giroux
Alex Tucker
Laurence Gonsalves
Kimme Utsi
Neil Drewett
Thomas Fortier
Andrew Montgomery
Tony Aksnes
Andreas Karlsson
Tomer Bar-Shlomo
Andrew Wild
Vladimiro Macedo
Jonathan Schmidt
Marc Burkhardt

Even Scharning
Leighton Brown
Jason Frisvold
Johan Fonden
Werner Schoeller
Jean Pierre Philippe
Simon Belmont
Paul Francis
James P Hobbs
Paul Bishop
Bruce Murphy
Panagiotis Govotsos
Hans Wezenberg
Robert Wagoner
Andrea Callea
Yannick Batista
Bill Adams
Magnus Johansson
Vaclav Simek
Tim Jenness
Steve Badcock
Jan Stoltenberg-Lerche
Mara Johannes
Terry Moore
Andrew Hayes
Alexis Delgado
Andreas Glaser
Kevin Rutten
Mike Vasconcellos
Michael Steil
Tom Hek
Timothy Berry
Jake Harvey
Anthony Becker
Robert Sherbine
Pauli Vaara
Michael Paschetag
Sami Rautiainen
Patrice Pelissier
Jack Murphy
Kolja Sennack
Joe Saint
Andreas Millinger
Sean Rider
David Diener
Dimitris Gourlis

Nicolai Kragh-Hansen
Ross Taylor
Rolf Hass
Justin Cooney
Martin Erhardsen
Glenn Larsson
Paul Hibbitts
Lorenzo Perugini
Hugh Cowan
Rafael Torres Lopez
Keith Burke
David Gaunt
Will Morton
Joerg Schlimm
Shawn Holtom
Ross Main
Bruce Canu
Mr. Daniel M. Gadze
Zoltáin Bãszãrmãnyi
Cedies
Anthony Olver
Mirko Holzer
Chris Morris
Alexandre El Boueri
Michal Klimek
Matthew Hohlfeld
Matt Shively
Stefano Ferilli
Steven Feurer
Patrick Kramer
Jonas Larsson
Johnnie Wallgren
Bruno Fonseca
Jeff Lowe
Gary Fisher
Torsten Schumacher
Henning Naarlien-Tolpinrud
Pesti Ferenc
J Brunner
Kim Sand
Vandeborre
Sven Rey
Phil Skelton
Dave Chamberlain
Michael Paull
Dan Duda

Paublo Smith
Duane Blacker
David Powell
Murat
Robert Martine-Mcevoy
Pepijn Vossen
Jeffrey L Murri
Christian Justesen
Stefan Lãtjen
Mark Short
Paul Corr
Werner Parzmayr
Marco Jirasek
Daniel Neugebauer
Gianluca Clos
Winton Mann
Kevin Unangst
Freddy Groen
Brandon Munger
Charlie Berglund
Torsten Kracke
John Hoggard
Rene Reichardt
Marcin W. Dä...Browski
Brian Cheng
Brandon Staggs
Eric Clark
Theodore Slicer Jr
Eric Chaney
Leszek Wolnik
Veli-Pekka Peltola
David R. Schaller
Tomas Lanquist
Brad Bidnick
Mark Jordan Sztainbok
Dennis Tollaksen
Marianne Eriksson
Marko S.K. Polvisalo
Michael Hansen
Francis G. Loch
Kenneth Sivertsem
Francesco Semeraro
Andre Fachat
Scott Allen
Leonard Powers
Germä¡n Quintero

Jeremy Richards
Stãphane Ghenne
Tom Lantz
Joanie K Raisovich
Jason M Jackson
Simon Ampts
Johannes Van Roest Dahl
Greg Gerke
Caelyn Mcaulay
Tony Aitken
Wetteronline Gmbh
Juri Laihonen
Pedro Rocha
Spirin Alexander
Michael Schreiber
Chris Swan
Sami Kuivamãki
Andrew Fisher
Roy Fielding
Christian Boettcher
Sean Connolly
Erik "Gronkh" Range
Jon Douglas
James Sachs
Dave Lewald
Peter Weuffen
Rodolfo Martell
Anthony Quinn
Mike Parker
Henrik Magnusson
Jonas Jacobsson
Pawel Czepo Czebotarewicz
Inge Strand
Warren Pilkington
Ronald Nicholson
Anthony Porrazza
Darren Glenn
Bjarte Kvalheim
David Wilson
David Isherwood
Mark Stacey
Andrew Baxter
Andrew Gowans
Volker Lerch
Maria Engstrã
Rob Napier

Chad Dylan Long
Jonny Hansen
David Raistrick
Mark Goddard
Marco Van Den Hout
Stuart Jarvis
Christian Vogelgsang
Paul S Cook
Andy (@R2D2Andy) Lockett
Tobias Karlsson
Andreas Andersson
Johan Wahlstrã
Rob Clarke
Barrie Tingle
Mika Myllyvaara
Ãyvind Lindahl
Fredrik Bjãrnsen
Wade Whiteman
Tobias Bjorndal
Chance Davis
Thomas Fuchs
Chris James
Matthias Liebich
David G Pruitt
Chris Howard
Damian Raschka
Martijn Bosschaart
Jim Causey
Martin Karlsson
Flemming Didriksen
Volker Gãrtner
G Sollich
Janne Alapeteri
Jeremiah Monzon
Matthew Rennie
Jason Fairchild
Joachim Schulze
Martin Gotthelf Jakobsen
Tim Bates
Arkadiusz Bronowicki
Henrik Wetterstrã
Zeljko Levanic
Robert Schultz
Vassilios Katsimpas
Uffe Jakobsen
Christoph Habbe

Bruno Fabietti
Geophrey Parry
Kevin Hughes
Mauro Sanna
James Barnhart
George Almpanidis
Mark Barrett
Howard Knibbs
Andrew Seeger
Simon Hadlington
Bernd Quermann
David Barnett
Frank Arlt
Monsieur Yves Grethen
Corey Meredith
Kenneth Whelan
Thomas Ally
Stephen Morgan
Craig Kohler
Colin Walker
Bryan Pope
Jonathan Clifton
Hākan Jonsson
Fabrizio Pedrazzini
John Ioannou
Peter Mattsson
Xavier Bodenand
Terrence Crossley
Dirk Ziegert
Ferdinand Schober
Udo Van Den Berg
Cameron Jackson
Matthias Lamm
Steven Innell
Roland Voāÿ
Jean-Francois Reynes
Hans-Petter Ruud
Ross Mckinlay
Paola Malfatto
Johan Bentzen
Lars Vandenbergh
Pcs Gmbh
Proskauer Rose Llp
Ernst Gunnar Gran
Hector Cid
Sascha Glade

Steve Rasmussen
Chanal Cedric
Omar Suleman
Jon Bowen
Tamā¡s Mechle
John Karatsoreos
Chris Dickerson
Christer Holmberg
Keith Buswell
Tor Johan Vatnehol
Christopher Harris
Kwok Chi Leong
Erkan Moustafa
Oscar Gurvitsch
Forrest Nettles
Henry Rivera
Balazs Szaszak
Adam O'brien
Frantisek Fris
Kai Engelbrecht
Simon Stokes
Tobias Hultman
Stefan Rotermund
Scott Devaney
Lukasz Hankus
Michael Maiwald
Peter Guyan
Kevin Bullock
Giambattista Mantuano
Daniel Riemslag
Sebastian Bergmann
Seppo Seppālā
Paul Martin
Mark Brown
Carl Musser
Andreas Feese
Alejandro Ramos Arizpe
Brian Eddy
James Higginbotham
Jim Drew
Ray Gillespie
Stefan Hammerer
Ionwalk Gmbh
Sarmad Gilani
Tolga Oraltay
George Pantazis

Arnold Blueml
Robert Bernardo
Anders Jensen
Giuseppe Chillemi
Lars Tremmel